FATHER
MYCHAL
JUDGE

FATHER
MYCHAL
JUDGE

AN
AUTHENTIC
AMERICAN
HERO

MICHAEL FORD

PAULIST PRESS
New York • Mahwah, N.J.

Cover quote from Rudolph Giuliani, former mayor of New York, in *Reader's Digest*, July 2002, p. 104.

Excerpts from *Bonaventure: The Soul's Journey into God, The Tree of Life, The Life of St. Francis*, translation and introduction by Ewert Cousins; preface by Ignatius Brady, The Classics of Western Spirituality, copyright © 1978 by Paulist Press, Inc., New York/Mahwah, N.J. Used with permission of Paulist Press. *www.paulistpress.com*.

"Canticle of Brother Sun" from Marion A. Habig, ed., *St. Francis of Assisi: Writings and Early Biographies, English Omnibus of the Sources for the Life of St. Francis* (Chicago: Franciscan Herald Press, 1972).

The Twelve Steps and a brief excerpt from *Alcoholics Anonymous* are reprinted with permission of Alcoholics Anonymous World Services, Inc. (A.A.W.S). Permission to reprint the Twelve Steps and a brief excerpt from *Alcoholics Anonymous* does not mean that A.A.W.S necessarily agrees with the views expressed herein. A.A. is a program of recovery from alcoholism *only* — use of the Twelve Steps in connection with programs and activities which are patterned after A.A., but which address other problems, or in any other non-A.A. context, does not imply otherwise. Although Alcoholics Anonymous is a spiritual program, A.A. is not a religious program, and use of A.A. material in the present connection does not imply A.A.'s affiliation with or endorsement of any sect, denomination, or specific religious belief.

The A.A. Preamble is reprinted with permission of the A.A. Grapevine, Inc.

"Breaking New Land," from *The Edge of Glory* by David Adam (Triangle/SPCK) used with permission.

The friendship blessing is taken from *Anam Cara* by John O'Donohue (New York: Harper-Collins Publishers, 1997; London: Bantam Press/Transworld Publishers, 1999). Used with permission.

Jacket design by Stefan Killen Design
Jacket photograph: AP/Wide World Photos

Library of Congress Cataloging-in-Publication Data

Ford, Michael.
    Father Mychal Judge : an authentic American hero / Michael Ford.
       p. cm.
    Includes bibliographical references.
    ISBN 0-8091-0552-7
    1. Judge, Mychal, 1933–2001. I. Title.
    BX4705.J767 F67 2002
    282'.092 – dc21   2002009475

Published by Paulist Press
997 Macarthur Boulevard
Mahwah, New Jersey 07430

www.paulistpress.com

Printed and bound in the United States of America

To the memory of those who lost their lives
on September 11, 2001,
and to those who grieve for them

Be patient in trials, watchful in prayer,
and never cease working.

—St. Francis of Assisi

CONTENTS

Part IV
SERAPHIC LOVE

PREFACE

———— ∞∞∞ ————

L IKE MANY PEOPLE THE WORLD OVER, I first learned of Father Mychal Judge through a picture. The Reuters photograph, showing his body being carried by five rescue workers from the dust and rubble of the North Tower, became an icon of September 11. It was likened even to Michelangelo's Pietà of Mary, the mother of Jesus, holding her son's slumped body at the foot of the cross. It was a heroic image of a man who had been born a first twin and now had died in the womb of the first twin tower. Father Judge's twin sister, Dympna Jessich, told reporters: "He was a hero who lived a glorious life — and he had a glorious death."

As I studied a color reproduction of the picture, emblazoned across the front page of a newspaper in Britain, I found myself drawn to the figure at the center. This modern crucifixion scene haunted me for days. I kept returning to the photograph to ponder its deeper meaning and, as a journalist specializing in the spiritual, began to wonder about the outer and inner lives of its subject.

The fact that we shared the same Christian name (albeit with different spellings) appealed to my sense of synchronicity. But only days later did I realize there was in fact a much more mysterious connection. One afternoon at my home in England, I opened an e-mail from a person I had once interviewed in the United States. He had been a close friend of Mychal Judge. The message informed me that, during the last weeks of his life, Father Mychal had been reading my book *Wounded Prophet,* a portrait of one of America's most prolific spiritual writers, Henri J. M. Nouwen. The friend had given him the book as a gift. Although the Franciscan friar tended to give away presents to needier souls, this one he kept. As he started to savor it over the summer of 2001, he apparently felt he was reading his own story.

While they came from vastly different backgrounds and ministered in contrasting contexts, both Catholic priests were prayerful extroverts who spoke from the heart and focused so intently on the needs of others that individuals felt cloaked by their presence. They were gifted men who allowed God to transfigure their struggles so they could bring hope and encouragement every step of the way. Both had healed through their wounds.

Mychal Judge identified so much with the book that it rekindled an interest in contracting a ghostwriter to help him pen an autobiography. It would have been a particularly frank account of his sixty-eight years, for he had experienced recovery from alcoholism and had grown through a transformed understanding of his priestly identity.

But it was not to be. A month later, newspapermen, radio broadcasters, and television reporters were piecing together his obituary multimedia style. They highlighted the fact that the fire chaplain's living and dying had been characterized by self-sacrifice in the service of others.

Although the World Trade Center attacks could not have been anticipated, Father Mychal was not unprepared for death. Failing health had predisposed him to bequeathing boxes of books from his sparsely furnished third-floor room at the friary in midtown Manhattan. On August 11, exactly a month before the disaster, he wrote to a friend: "Would you have these few books so that when I go to 'My Isle in Heaven' I'll know they are in good hands?"

When grief-stricken friends entered his high-ceilinged room on West Thirty-first Street on September 12, they were surprised to find it looking even more austere than usual. But there, in the spartan setting, lay a text, alone on the dresser. Mychal Judge had evidently been reading *Wounded Prophet* shortly before his death. A bookmark lay within the middle pages.

Invited by Paulist Press to write about another wounded healer, I began to enter the world of a legendary New Yorker whose heroism, I soon discovered, had been all the more remarkable for the difficulties he had striven to overcome in his personal life. This impressionistic portrait is drawn from many exclusive interviews with his friends who in places tell their own stories. It is offered both as a tribute and a testimony to a one-time alcoholic who could never shake off his strongest addiction: a love for other people.

June 1, 2002

ACKNOWLEDGMENTS

Aﬀ FTER INTERVIEWING FRIENDS of Father Mychal Judge, O.F.M. (Order of Friars Minor), in England during the winter of 2001, I arrived in New York to continue my research in the spring-time — exactly six months after the attacks. The day I landed, the flag-draped body of another firefighter was being carried from the rubble of the World Trade Center. To that date, 159 of the 343 fire-fighters and paramedics who perished had been found; the official death toll from the attacks stood at 2,830; more than 15,000 body parts had been recovered and the remains of 753 victims estab-lished. An additional 1,919 death certificates had been issued to families in cases where a body had not been identified.

This was the backdrop to my assignment in a city I had reported from in happier times. On this occasion I was there during Holy Week. It seemed appropriate to stand silently at Ground Zero on Good Friday, reflecting on the witness of Father Mychal Judge and his fellow American heroes. It was in this context of desolation and continuing grief that I began interviewing New Yorkers who had known the now world-famous friar. I should like to thank all those who were prepared to talk about him at a time when the memories of September 11 were still acutely painful. I am grateful to the friends who entrusted me with contact numbers and addresses so I could broaden and deepen my understanding of the priest's life and to those members of his order at St. Francis of Assisi Friary with whom I had conversations.

I should like to express gratitude to Father Michael Evernden and the Paulist community on Fifty-ninth Street for their generous hospitality during my stay. It was heaven to roll out of bed and into the 7:30 Mass, said daily with such prayerfulness in the tranquil chapel. I felt particularly upheld by our reflections over the high-fiber breakfast table and the shorter conversations in the elevator between floors.

The encouragement and kindness of Father Lawrence Boadt, publisher at Paulist Press, has been especially welcome. It has been a particular privilege to have worked with my editor, Paul McMahon, whose quiet professionalism, understanding, and sensitivity kept the project on track. Paul's assistant, Barbara McCormick, has also been a delight, efficiently liaising with contributors and tracking down elusive contacts with pains-taking care. Thanks also to copy editor John Eagleson, marketing manager Robert Welsch, publicist Jill Gleichman, and network administrator Dave Titus. I am particularly grateful to Stephen Weaver and David Torevell for reading the manuscript so meticu-lously and giving such insightful feedback. Special thanks to Tim Pike for gently encouraging me to write the book and for his enthusiastic support of the project.

Many others have been thoughtful, helpful, and kind, among them my mother, Margaret, and brother, Nigel; and John Dear, Audrey and Dick Cox, Richard Edwards, Maria-Alicia Ferrera-Pena, Eva Heymann, Vince Hunt, Peter Huxham, Tom Jordan, Giles Legood, Lynda Morgan, Melanie Phillips, Robert Plant, Diane Reid, Michael Smith, Andrew Taylor, Betty Taylor, Mark Warburton, Norman Winter, and Janet Wynn. Their interest is much appreciated.

Part One

ANGELS
AND DEMONS

Francis venerated with a very great affection the angels who are with us in our struggle and who walk *in the midst of the shadow of death* with us.

— Thomas of Celano, *The Second Life of St. Francis,*
chap. 149, no. 197

1

THE BRIDGE

⎯⎯∞⎯⎯

IT WAS A BALMY SUMMER'S NIGHT in Manhattan. The illuminated city looked seductive. Father Mychal Judge was in his usual good spirits. It was June 2001, and he had just returned to the city after attending the "Chapter of Mats," an old monastic tradition where friars gather to read from the Rule of St. Francis and discuss their life together. Father Mychal had driven back to the friary with the Franciscan preacher and writer Richard Rohr, who had flown in from New Mexico to address the meeting. In the car, Judge suddenly asked Rohr a question: "Can I take you on one of my favorite walks tonight?"

Richard Rohr had already arranged to spend the rest of the day with a priest friend from Long Island, Michael Holzmann. So Mychal Judge invited him along too. At 10:00 P.M., the two priests turned up at Father Mychal's room: "With loving eyes and a warm handshake, he welcomed me like a long-lost friend," Holzmann remembered. "He mocked Richard about being so famous and promised us his special tour. I could see out the window of his room that it overlooked the firehouse — that was where he parked his chaplain's car. I rode up front with Mychal, who explained that every cop and firefighter knew his vehicle."

The car sped downtown toward Brooklyn Bridge, which connects the island of Manhattan with Mychal Judge's native Brooklyn — two different worlds. The bridge, regarded as one of the greatest engineering feats, was opened in 1883 after fourteen years' construction and the loss of at least twenty-six lives. It could be seen as a spiritual symbol of Mychal Judge's New York ministry, linking diverse groups across the city. The car's fire department emblem allowed the chaplain to park anywhere. It was not unusual for him to switch on the siren and lights to entertain friends as he pretended to be on an emergency across the waterway. But that night he parked and walked, taking the tired but intrigued priests on an energetic tour. Like an experienced city guide, he could reel off grand statistics at the drop of a firefighter's helmet. The friends recounted how they had walked across the bridge and stopped to look back at the magnificent skyline. "He had this desire to show us, not only the bridge, but also all these other wonderful landmarks," Richard Rohr told me.

Mychal Judge laced his eulogy with precise statistics about all the buildings, especially the World Trade Center. Richard Rohr distinctly remembered his focusing on its measurements and features. Built by the Port Authority, the 110-story twin towers and the five-acre plaza beneath had been opened twenty-five years before. Father Mychal had watched them being built. He could recall how a rock climber had inched his way up one of them in a matter of hours and how they had once been used for a high-wire act. A year after he had joined the chaplaincy team of the New York Fire Department, terrorists had set off a bomb in an underground garage there. Six people had died. Mychal Judge had been on duty that day. Shaken New Yorkers felt an increased sense of vulnerability.

"We reminisced and theologized about New York," said Richard Rohr. "He clearly loved the whole city immensely, its people and its architectural achievements too. I cannot remember that we saw more than the rising towers in the distance. They were on the other side of Manhattan Island, but still awesome in their perspective."

That night, three months before the World Trade Center attacks, Father Mychal repeatedly commented on the beauty of the panorama and how fortunate they were to stand there and appreciate it. It was his favorite cityscape, one he liked to share. "There is something for me about the Brooklyn Bridge — I must walk it at least once a week," Mychal Judge had told a reporter.

"I walk from the friary downtown, then across the bridge, and maybe keep going out to Brighton Beach. I get an ice cream cone there and then come home. I get ideas on the Brooklyn Bridge even when I'm not looking for one.... I love to look at the Statue of Liberty, the lights of the city, the Verrazano Bridge, the Manhattan Bridge carrying the subway cars. The city is just the most extraordinary place to live."

It was approaching midnight by the time the three men returned to the friary and retreated to their rooms. But as Mychal Judge prepared for sleep, his beeper went off: a fireman's father had died far north of the city. As weary as he was, the sixty-eight-year-old chaplain dashed back to his car and drove for more than an hour north of New York so he could offer sympathy and solace to the family. As Richard Rohr and Michael Holzmann ambled to their rooms and fell into bed, Mychal Judge sped off into the night.

The time on the bridge had seemed mysteriously holy and beautiful, even prophetic. Richard Rohr sensed it pointed to "an intuition about the special quality of that place," while Michael Holzmann wondered retrospectively if it would have been the last time Mychal Judge had viewed the towers "with such a sense of peace, serenity, and joy."

2

LAST RITES

—∞∞∞—

"**I**T IS GOING TO BE a beautiful day today — sunshine throughout. Low humidity. Really a splendid September day. The afternoon temperature about eighty degrees. Great weather for the primary election."

It was as promising as television forecasts got at that time of year. On September 11, 2001, the early morning sun glistened over the windows of the World Trade Center, where, on a normal weekday, up to 50,000 people could be at their desks and 140,000 tourists might be riding the elevators to the observation decks. Few suites were unoccupied. The tenants included 430 companies from 28 countries, a nerve center for banking, finance, insurance, import, export, custom brokerage, bond trading, and transportation. Work had begun at the site in 1966 and the towers had opened to the public in the 1970s. At the time of the 1993 bombing, a structural design engineer claimed each tower had been built to withstand the impact of a fully fueled 707 jet.

That fall morning, pilot's son and Franciscan priest Brian Carroll headed off from West Thirty-first Street, where he lived in community with Mychal Judge. Walking briskly east at a quarter to nine, Carroll suddenly noticed a plane flying unusually low near the tower blocks and wondered if a TV company were making an extravagant commercial. Turning on to Sixth Avenue and moving south, he heard "a deep noise that sounded like a train" and then watched in disbelief as the plane crashed into the north tower at an estimated speed of five hundred miles per hour. A fireball and clouds of gushing black smoke accompanied the muffled explosion. Shocked and trembling, Carroll rushed back to the friary and raced up to the third floor, banging on Mychal Judge's room and pushing the door open. The fire chaplain was sitting calmly, holding his head in his hands.

"Mychal — I just saw a plane fly into the World Trade Center," Carroll blurted.

"Oh, my God! Oh, my God!" Judge responded, intermingling this reaction with an earthier phrase or two. "You're kidding me."

"Mychal, honest to God. I have just seen this. It's unbelievable."

"Oh, my God, oh, my God." Judge repeated the expression like a mantra but was interrupted by his beeper. This was no joke. Carroll wished his friend luck as the priest quickly changed into his heat-resistant uniform and ran out of the building with the words "I think they need you" ringing in his ears. He crossed to the Engine 1/Ladder 24 firehouse to get his car. Captain Danny Brethel, who had just finished a twenty-four-hour shift, offered to drive him down. Neither was to return.

The New York Fire Department mobilized hundreds of firefighters from Lower Manhattan, who were joined by units from across the five boroughs. Tyrone Johnson remembered seeing Father Mike outside the burning World Trade Center. As clouds of choking smoke obliterated an azure sky, flames licked their way across the towers. People on fire jumped to their deaths. It was reminiscent of a scene from Dante's *Inferno*.

"When we pulled to our command post, Father Mike was standing there with the chiefs, looking at what was going on," said Tyrone Johnson. "He was standing there comforting people as he would normally do. He was very serious. I had never seen such a grim look on his face. It was one of sorrow. He was really upset. I was standing five feet away from him at the time. As people were jumping out the buildings, you could see him praying for them."

One of the first to speak with the chaplain was the mayor of New York, Rudolph Giuliani. As Father Mike ran by, Giuliani put a hand on his shoulder: "Mychal, please pray for us." With a big, but anxious, Irish smile, he replied: "I always do." Then he ran on with the firefighters into the lobby of the north tower.

Never one to flinch from danger, Father Mike was there to offer solidarity to the firefighters. Unlike the rest of the world, they had no wider perspective of the unfolding story. Film-maker Jules Naudet, who happened to be at the center making a documentary on a trainee firefighter, shot unique footage. He had to stay close to battalion chief Joe Pfeifer, who had set up a command center to coordinate the rescue effort. The camera captured the pandemonium surrounding fire chiefs as they scrambled together their rescue plan. Their looks were not of fear but of incredulity and uncertainty.

The explosions blew out and splintered lobby windows. Some of those who leapt from the floors above crashed fatally into the remaining panes. Flaming jet fuel had shot straight through the elevator shaft. The elevators had stopped. The firefighters had to lug hose and equipment weighing more than sixty pounds up the stairs. Each flight took a minute to climb. The tower's internal communication system had shut down so the men had to rely on their own radios. Despite the chaos, there was a calmness and orderliness about the operation.

Jules Naudet filmed Father Mike in the lobby. Usually smiling to give the firefighters encouragement, he looked pale and preoccupied, praying and pacing, a lone spiritual presence amid the confusion and the conflagration. Some suggested he was saying the rosary. His white Roman collar seemed to stand out in the blackness of the hour. Occasionally his eyes looked up, as if toward heaven. "I could tell he was praying," said one firefighter. "Father Judge would at least make eye contact with you and give you a reassuring look. This was not occurring — almost like he knew this was not good."

Eyewitnesses described the collapse of the south tower, the second one to be hit, as being "a scene from hell accompanied by a horrendous sound — like a locomotive tearing through the building." Then a strange silence seemed to descend and hover over streets carpeted by glass shards, bricks, and twisted metal.

Fears grew about the fate of the burning north tower, which was still standing. Early accounts suggested that when Father Mike removed his helmet to pray the last rites over a dying firefighter (who had been crushed by a falling body), he was struck on the back of the head by flying debris and died. There would, however, have been no sacramental reason for his taking off the helmet. But one firefighter remembered seeing the chaplain standing upright by the emergency command post and later in the lobby that was plunged into darkness when the South Tower collapsed. Christian Waugh told journalists: "I'm assuming he gave last rites to the guy in Company 216 and then ran into the lobby, because I was with him in that lobby. He was standing there a few feet from me."

Another report revealed that when Father Mike had been urged to leave the building, he had said: "I'm not finished here." Through the smoke and dust, Jules Naudet trained the light on his camera on the rescue operation. Amid the confusion of the scene, he was asked to tilt the light downward because a man had been injured. He was lying at the base of the elevator. Suddenly the light irradiated a white clerical collar. It was Father Mike. A firefighter opened the priest's shirt and checked for a pulse. But "he was gone."

Eventually five rescue workers, including Lieutenant Billy Cosgrove, of the Manhattan Traffic Task Force, carried the body out through the rubble. It was at that moment that photographer Shannon Stapleton focused her lens on a tableau of pathos, a haunting picture that was to become iconic of the entire disaster. The body was placed on the corner of Church Street and Vesey Street in front of the burning towers.

The area was evacuated. People giving running commentaries to their friends on their mobile phones started running for their lives. The smell of acrid smoke and the sound of piercing screams overpowered the senses. From the ground, the sky looked gray. It resembled nuclear snow or volcanic ash. "It was hard to see and hard to breathe — my eyes and lungs were burning," said New York City police officer José Alfonso Rodríguez, who was helping with the evacuations when he suddenly spotted "a commotion" at the corner of Church and Vesey, where a body was lying close to a burned-out ambulance. When he first saw the figure in dark trousers, he thought it was a fellow police officer.

"Can somebody get this man a priest? Can somebody get this man a priest?" screamed Lieutenant Cosgrove.

Rodríguez said he knew a church nearby.

"Son, can you try to find this man a priest?"

Rodríguez told me how he had raced one block north, dodging burning debris and falling bodies. He went into St. Peter's Catholic Church, where he spied a woman tearing up linen: "I asked if there were any priests around, but they were all out. I said we needed a priest to give somebody the last rites. The lady asked if I was Catholic. I said I was. She said I could give last rites in an emergency. I was really shocked to hear this. I ran back down the street and over to the lieutenant. I put my arm on him and told him what the lady had said. I asked him if he too was Catholic, and he said he was." Rodríguez offered to pray with Cosgrove. The two policemen walked over to the body. A black jacket shrouded the head.

> We knelt down. I grabbed Father Judge's hand and the lieutenant put his hand on the priest's head. We were still looking up at the burning north tower. We said a quick Our Father and a Glory Be. I think the lieutenant said, "Ashes to ashes, dust to dust." I felt like an altar boy again. My heart was pumping out of my chest because my adrenalin rates were running so high. After praying over the body, we got back up and gave each other a little hug. We left the body right there. It just looked like he was sleeping. I did not know what his injury was. I had never met the man and did not know his name, but I had seen him on emergencies before.
>
> We both went back into the north tower and inside the lobby again. People were screaming. "The building's moving.

The building's moving. Get out! Get out!" We ran out into
the plaza again. We started walking away. We looked up.
The sky was pitch black. It looked like a ceiling with smoke
pouring out. We couldn't see the top of the tower and the
blue sky beyond it. We just saw the building opening up
and all the smoke. Then it started collapsing. For a second,
the smoke cleared, and I saw the tower antennas move. I
knew it was coming down. I ran. Stuff was hitting us in the
back. Glass was flying. Huge chunks of debris were falling
all around us, and there was fire.

I hid inside a building that itself was burning. With the
tower coming down, I thought that was it. There's no way
we're getting out. I'm going to die here. It seemed like the
end of the earth. I wasn't scared at all up until the collapse
of the north tower. It imploded and landed on Vesey and
West Street. If the tower had fallen east, I would have been
crushed.

But we had a guardian angel that took care of us. The
lieutenant and I think Father Judge smiled down on us and
made sure we got out.

A bond grew between the two men. They discussed whether,
as lay people, it had been legitimate to perform this "last rites"
ceremony. "I talked to a bishop who was sent as an emissary from
the pope himself," Rodríguez explained. "He said technically I
couldn't give last rites, but then he began to get emotional. He
knew Father Judge and said it was the greatest thing we could
have done."

The impromptu ritual was, in fact, entirely in keeping with
Father Mychal's own sacramental theology of hallowing the
moment and was typical of the way ordinary people generated
light in the darkness of that day.

José Alfonso Rodríguez, who described himself as a lapsed
Catholic, found his own faith in God strengthened by the experience — yet it remained a mystery: "I am just a lowly cop. Why

me? Why was I there? How did I cross paths with this man? Why did the lieutenant scream for a priest when I was the one other cop there? Was it my Catholic calling?"

Rodríguez showed me what he had been wearing around his neck that day: a silver crucifix, a silver Jerusalem cross, and a silver medallion of St. Michael, patron saint of New York police officers. The words "Protect Us" were inscribed on the medallion. It was only afterward he had remembered about the chains. It was exactly the sort of spiritual connection that would have pleased Mychal Judge.

Firefighters took Father Mike's body to St. Peter's Church, where it was laid in front of the altar. They covered it with a white cloth and placed his stole, helmet, and chaplain's badge on top. Then they knelt and prayed. The fire chaplain had laid down his life for his friends, the ultimate mark of Christian discipleship. The friar from "Manhattan 10001" was classed as the first registered victim of the attacks. His death certificate was 00001, a posthumous honor for a New Yorker whose proud boast was that he dwelt in "the greatest city in the world."

Back at the friary, friends were already sensing the worst. Brian Carroll, who had been the first to break the news of the attack that morning, stood outside St. Francis Church with a colleague. They looked at each other, and he said: "Something bad has happened to Mychal." At that moment the pastor, Father Peter Brophy, and another friar came through the doors and, with neither a word nor a glance, walked by and headed across the street to the firehouse. A few hours later the body, dressed in its white sheet, was brought back to the firehouse and laid out on a table. Friars gathered around, praying and crying.

"My first thought on leaving the firehouse was 'My God, it's all over,'" Carroll recalled. "I actually felt a sense of peace and comfort for Mychal. I actually laughed as I caught the eyes of one of the other friars and said, 'This is how he would have scripted the end.' The silence of the streets, now almost completely empty on this beautiful September day, mirrored the silence in my heart."

There was a stillness on West Thirty-first Street. Carroll looked up at the windows of Mychal Judge's room and thought: "You're at peace now." His struggles and anxieties, his "worrying about doing the right thing and obsessing" were also laid to rest that day. He died doing what he loved to do — being alongside others in need. Such natural compassion had always given him moments of freedom from his own inner demons. Mychal Judge had always stood shoulder to shoulder with other pilgrims in life — the frightened, the confused, and the battle weary. Now he was at peace and perhaps, for the first time, was experiencing what it was like to be on the receiving end of his own brand of unconditional love.

A photograph of Father Mike was posted at a sidewalk shrine outside the firehouse, alongside pictures of the local firefighters who had lost their lives. Father Brophy commented: "There is a lot of sadness because this is a tremendous loss, but the manner in which Mychal died is also a great honor because he died in service. As a friar I'm honored by who he was and how he reached out to people, no matter who they were."

It seemed, however, that it was indeed a death he would have chosen. As Stephen Weaver, a priest friend in London, watched the pictures on television, he instinctively knew Mychal Judge would have been at the center of the disaster:

> I began to fear that he was indeed caught up in it and, when news came of his death, I was strangely unsurprised. The manner of his passing was entirely in keeping with the manner of his life — high profile, dynamic, heroic, and self-sacrificial. There was something Christlike about the way in which his death was a transcending of the disaster. It has since given people a great sense of inspiration that this person, who was a victim, is also someone who can be claimed as a hero and, in some senses, a saint. Heroic virtue was demonstrated by Mychal on that day in a way that redeems the evil of the event itself.

Stephen Weaver later reflected ironically that, if Mychal Judge had not been killed at the base of the twin towers that day, he would have been "furious with himself," given his absolute dedication to duty. He would have wanted to be fully part of the experience, one shared not only by the firefighters he was ministering to, but by his city and country. "As the events unfolded, all the world's cameras were already fixed on that place. As if in a drama, Mychal walked into the heat of the action and performed that heroic act. He would have been pleased to think this was the case. Even as he was losing his life, he was gaining this sense of a fitting end, placing the Franciscan spirit and Christian love at the heart of the tragedy."

Others who had known him only fleetingly were equally reflective. Michael Holzmann remembered the evening, just three months before, when they had stood admiring the lights of New York from Brooklyn Bridge: "I immediately recalled that beautiful night on the bridge. I was aware that his smile was coming from the depth of his heart. That which had made up a beautiful scene had now become the center of horror and terror. But, for all that, I knew I had shared one page in the book of a great man."

Accompanied by two friars, Father Mychal's body was taken by ambulance that evening from the firehouse to a morgue on First Avenue. It was later conveyed to a funeral home, where it was embalmed. On the afternoon of Thursday, September 13, the funeral director brought the body to the lower church of St. Francis where a public viewing took place until a wake service the following evening. Afterward the body was transferred to the upper church for a funeral Mass.

3

THE WAY TO LOVE

—◦◦◦◦—

HE FRIARS OBEYED his final wishes. As the last expression of
his vows of poverty and humility, they laid his body on the
bare ground. Then they washed him, anointed him with spice, and
dressed him in a habit. Candles and incense were lit round his bed.
After he had been placed in his coffin on the day of his funeral,
the crowd headed toward the parish church. Led by the local
clergy, the friars acted as pallbearers. A crow flew overhead. Rich
landowners, entire families, poor beggars, and cripples followed.
As the trumpets and drums sounded, they waved their flags and
olive branches and joined in the singing.

Mychal Judge could recount this story about the death of Francis of Assisi — indeed, the life of the saint had inspired him
throughout his earthly pilgrimage. Francis (1182–1226) saw himself as God's troubadour or fool. The son of an affluent cloth
merchant of Assisi, Italy, he became a junior partner in the family business. But he gained a reputation as a young playboy and
one who desired social status. In 1202 Francis was taken pris-
oner during a war between Assisi and neighboring Perugia. He
was freed after a year, returning home to question his former lifestyle. He began to find himself drawn to a life of penance that
included periods of deep prayer, almsgiving, and pilgrimages. An
encounter with a leper led to his working among the social outcasts of his day. His volte-face provoked an acrimonious conflict
with his father, which reached a climax in 1206. In response to
what he perceived to be a vocation from God to rebuild the ruined
chapel of San Damiano, Francis stole some expensive cloth from
the family store to raise money for the project. His father brought

him to trial, after which Francis stripped naked and renounced his heritage in a dramatic scene before the local bishop. He then spent several years living as a penitent hermit caring for lepers and restoring small chapels in the area.

In 1208, Francis intuited a deeper calling to rebuild the wider church: he started preaching publicly as a means of living out Jesus' mission to the apostles: "Go and proclaim this message: The kingdom of heaven is near. Heal the sick, bring the dead back to life, cleanse the lepers, and drive out demons. You received this as a gift, so give it as a gift" (Matt 10:7–8). Attracting his first followers, Francis gave birth to a new movement. Within a year there were twelve brothers. Drawing on a number of gospel texts, Francis encapsulated their way of life in a short statement, which the group took to Rome to secure tentative approval from Pope Innocent III. These Friars Minor ("Lesser Brothers") returned to Assisi and set up community in a rural chapel from which they started to spread out in small bands throughout central Italy. They prayed contemplatively, worked as laborers, and preached, calling people to conversion by their own word and example. Francis had a deep affinity for all of creation, epitomized in a sermon to the birds.

In 1212, a young aristocratic woman from Assisi, Clare, joined the movement with several other women, founding their own community of "Poor Ladies." Francis, meanwhile, guided groups of devout lay men and women called the Brothers and Sisters of Penance, known later as the "Third Order." The preaching ministry of the friars extended beyond Italy: Francis was convinced that God intended their witness to be worldwide.

At the chapter of 1217, he inaugurated missions beyond the Alps and to the Crusader states in the Near East. Francis had yearned to preach the message of Christ to Muslims and win therefore a martyr's death. He walked over the Pyrenees barefoot, was shipwrecked, and in 1219 arrived in Egypt, where Crusaders were mounting an attack on the forces of Sultan al-Kamil. Francis succeeded in meeting the Sultan who, although remaining unconverted, was impressed by the obvious sincerity of the friar. However, by now there were tensions back home among the brotherhood, which numbered three thousand. Francis returned to Italy to find disagreements and divisions over the future direction of the order. He also had to face real opposition and rejection from the clerical hierarchy, suspicious of a movement whose profile was increasing. This forced him to resign the administration of the order and seek the appointment of a sympathetic cardinal to protect the movement. Nonetheless, Francis continued to be respected as the spiritual head of the brotherhood. He revised the rule, which met with full papal approval in 1223. However, during these years, Francis suffered serious illness and withdrew for long periods of prayer. While on retreat on Mount La Verna in 1224, he had a profound mystical experience in which he received the wounds of Christ's passion imprinted on his hands, feet, and side, the first recorded case of the stigmata. Two years after his death in 1226, he was canonized. He has since been described as the only perfect Christian after Jesus.

St. francis of assisi was a role model for Mychal Judge, whose own life bore all the spiritual hallmarks of a disciple of Francis. For the last fifteen years of his life, he resided permanently at the friary attached to St. Francis of Assisi Church in midtown Manhattan. Founded in 1844, it became known as "the heart of New York," offering a sacramental life for Catholics from throughout the metropolitan area and reaching out into the wider community as a refuge of nourishment and hope for the poor and disadvantaged.

It was originally a parish church, but by the 1920s the neighborhood had become commercialized and most of the residents had moved out. St. Francis was the first in Holy Name Province to be classed a "service church" as well as a parish of the Archdiocese of New York. Its ministry focused on providing devotional services all day long to the local populace, which largely included shoppers, workers, and tourists from many different ethnic backgrounds.

The church became famous for its care of the hungry through the St. Francis Breadline, which began in 1930 during the Great Depression and has not missed a day since. As worshipers line up inside the church to receive the broken body of Christ in the host, the homeless queue up outside to receive their daily bread. Every June 13, the feast day of St. Anthony, eighty thousand loaves are blessed by the friars and distributed. Devotions to this canonized friend of the poor take place every Tuesday. During the war, St. Francis became known as "the Confession Church" — eight hundred thousand confessions (more than two thousand a day) were heard there in 1944 alone. With the sacrament of reconciliation available twelve hours a day, seven days a week, daily confessions in Father Mychal's time numbered 450.

Between forty and fifty friars were in residence; half were on the staff. Father Mychal felt at home in such an environment. Imbued with the spirit of St. Francis himself, he knew he was a member of a fraternity that cared for others. There was an equilibrium about its spiritual life. Community prayers, celebrations of the Eucharist, and devotions to Mary and the saints were complemented around the clock by outreach programs to feed the hungry, support immigrants, care for the mentally ill, or give practical help and encouragement to the children of homeless families. There was also a commitment to moving from a ministry of charity toward a ministry of justice, a rhythm with which he felt in tune.

Father Mychal began his day beside his bed, remembering people by name. He once described his morning ritual: "The first thing I do each day is get down on my knees and pray, 'Lord, take me where you want me to go, let me meet who you want me to meet, tell me what to say, and keep me out of your way.' He'll show me how. But I learn. I make mistakes. Life is a learning process. I learn from people — I watch and listen."

He undertook his spiritual exercises while inhaling the aroma of percolating coffee. "He had a special blend that he got at an uptown supermarket because the guy who made the coffee had customers at the firehouse," a friar disclosed. "He would get six bags for the price of two, so there was a little corruption going on. He was in on that deal and knew the coffee maker would always have a blend for him. He would tell me that this was the best coffee in the whole of New York. I asked why he didn't go to a closer supermarket. 'It's not as good,' he would reply. Mychal had a Brooklyn expression: 'You get the good coffee and the bad coffee. You get the good gas and the bad gas. You get a good roll and a bad roll.' "

An Irish American troubadour who could burst into a rendition of "Paddy McGinty's Goat" as spontaneously as he could bless a drug addict in Central Park, Mychal Judge was a spiritual tour de force in the materialistic grid of New York City with as many orbits of influence as he seemed to have friends. Ministering across all lines of race, social status, gender, and faith, he was first and foremost the people's priest.

While he prayed constantly, he did not cast himself in the mold of a calm, contemplative religious brother. The good works of Father Mike, to which thousands bear testimony, often found expression in action, drama, and headline-making circumstances, such as the TWA crash off Long Island. As a Catholic chaplain with the New York Fire Department, the frontline Franciscan had a scanner, pager, and a private line in his room. Whenever the emergency was "a three- or four-alarm fire," he would be notified, but, if it were a field fire or warehouse blaze, he would not be expected to be on the scene. He had a particular rapport with the older fire dispatchers at the 911 headquarters, who would advise him on whether or not he ought to head out to a particular fire. He would get beeped throughout the day, but usually his priestly duties kicked in when the fires had been put out. If Father Mike could not be located in the friary, his brothers knew he would be at the bedside of an injured firefighter or praying with the young family of a crewman who had died.

But this was only part of the story. So many people called him to ask for advice or take services that often he returned at night to find up to forty messages flashing on the unit in his room.

Answering machines were a lifeline to him — and he usually burned them out within a year. As much as he complained about all the calls he would get, he would try to answer every one. This became Night Prayer for him. He might have had a call from an eighty-five-year-old woman who was alone or from a person who had just had a fight with a boyfriend. The calls had to be returned and the callers consoled, even prayed with on the line. People placed demands on him, but he never turned them away. Six months before his death, however, he was forced to record a message on his machine, saying he could now manage baptisms, weddings, and funerals only for fire department personnel.

As he rushed in and out of the Franciscan complex in the shadow of the Empire State Building, Mychal Judge would glance up at the mosaic on the front tower of the church. It depicted St. Francis in heavenly glory with the saint's hometown of Assisi beneath his feet. In the foreground lay the basilica where he was buried. Above the mosaic was the Franciscan coat of arms. It showed a cross, in front of which were two overlaid arms with wounded hands: those of Christ and St. Francis. The interior of the church, with its many shrines and mosaics, was completely restored in Romanesque style and the sanctuary redesigned in 1992, the year Father Mychal became a fire chaplain.

St. Anthony's Shrine, beneath the upper church, was built in 1931 to cope with the influx of worshipers. Upon its inaugural blessing, it became the National Shrine of St. Anthony of Padua. It was there every morning that Father Mychal would join the community for prayers, mentioning firefighters, police, and all who held the city of New York together. If he subsequently met those he had named, he would tell them: "I prayed for you this morning." But there were always prayers of personal gratitude too. Father Francis Muller had particular memories of Father Mychal at morning prayer one day: "A couple of years ago, when we were thanking God for this and that, he said, 'I thank God for twenty-one years of sobriety.' I always remembered that."

He said Mass virtually every day and would often go to as many meetings of Alcoholics Anonymous as he could fit in during the week. They were held at various times all over the city and were often powerful, spiritual experiences for him. Back at the friary, Father Muller would pass his room at 10:00 P.M. on his way to the third-floor chapel. Mychal would often call out: "Tell Jesus I'll be into see him in a few minutes." Such an open response was "very much a faith statement," said Father Muller, who pointed out that, while Mychal Judge had his faults, they were all part of being a Franciscan: "He was definitely a good person, not pious, but very open and manly about everything."

Before bed he would remember friends by name again and write late-night notes on yellow cards, gifting other people with encouragement: "I would get them on my door all the time," recalled Brian Carroll. "If something had gone wrong that day or I was going through a difficult time, I would wake up to a supportive note under my door, always telling me not to worry. I hope I was also helpful to him in telling him not to worry."

Fellow Franciscans felt supported by his considerate demeanor. One recalled: "I came home complaining about a tough day at work. Mychal said, 'Tomorrow you'll wake up and Jesus will still love you.'" Another noted that he had never heard Mychal Judge speak an unkind word against a friar in all the years he had lived with him: "I think one of his strengths — and what led people to him — was that he bore no judgment or condemnation toward anyone. He was open and understanding, and he accepted people for what they were. He had that Franciscan gift of looking for the good in another, easily brushing away what was sometimes less than perfect."

But given the pressures of living in a community of men, and his own complex personality, it would have been surprising had there not been occasions when he clashed with others. Speaking to a friend outside the order about the pettiness of some friars, he once remarked: "This place drives me nuts."

In turn, some found *him* hard to live with. He could be opinionated and had strong convictions about how his community should "do things." He got into trouble for collecting clothing and cluttering the hallways. While always well intentioned, he created problems for the more pragmatic brothers. "He was also hard to live with in a good way," said Brian Carroll. "He was so comfortable with people and so comfortable with being himself, so open and honest about the person he was, about his loves, his cares, and his concerns, that he made other friars uncomfortable because he revealed to us our own deceit."

He often gave impromptu performances of Irish songs, but they were not always appreciated by the community. His incessant rendition of "Steve O'Donnell's Wake" once tried the patience of a group of friars who started throwing paper napkins at him. Mychal Judge was hurt by their reaction.

Richard Rohr confirmed that Mychal Judge had not been at ease with all his brothers: "My guess is his style and freedom may have been a point of envy for other people. I did not sense he drew his primary support system there, even though he didn't seem to be avoiding community or living outside of it. He really fitted the habit and was such a worthy hero."

Mychal Judge knew there were tensions within him about modern-day Franciscanism. Even though quick-fire wit over a community meal could resemble a scene from a Marx Brothers movie, it only fleetingly disguised substantial issues of power being played out at times between factions of the friary. He knew this merely mirrored Catholic life in New York City and its polarization of conservative and liberal voices in the church. This was particularly reflected in his relationship with the late archbishop of New York, Cardinal John O'Connor, whose conservatism jarred with his more liberal outlook.

Father Mychal was only too aware of the political backdrop to pastoral work in the city. He knew how to maneuver his way through the ecclesiastical labyrinth and play off the rival forces within his own community. But some friars failed to gauge the measure of the man and came to resent the fact that much of his ministry was mediated through public events that were often well reported and photographed. They also knew that institutional life could never fully contain their autonomous brother.

"Mychal was a free spirit. You could not tie him down," said Father Anthony McNeill, a friar in Britain and a close friend of Mychal Judge. "He moved where he felt there was a need. He wasn't an institutionalized friar. He didn't fall out of his bed and onto the altar linen. While some may have been content to live within the institutional structure, he wasn't. He had a sense of priority. While he had his own life to live, he knew also that he had to go out and find it with the people who might need him."

The restless Franciscan was the spiritual version of James Bond: "If you could get a friar action toy, Mychal would be the model," said McNeill. "He didn't sit in. He was a go-getter. That was his appeal, his charism, his magnetism." If Father Mychal could help someone in difficulty, he would take great pleasure in rushing over or telephoning back quickly to offer advice. But he had a keen awareness and sensitivity about counseling technique. He also liked celebrations and large gatherings where he seemed to draw people to him; he was less enthusiastic about wedding receptions because he found it hard to work the crowds.

The troubadour relished telling stories of how he believed the hand of God had been at work in his life, so that other people could be spurred on to search for God in their own situations. He had an overwhelming sense of having been blessed by God. When the fire department gave him his car, for instance, he was touched because he felt it expressed the staff's love and respect for him. He said he didn't deserve some of the presents he received, even though they came endlessly. He would always pass them on.

Despite his popularity, he found it hard to understand why people were attracted to him. "What have I got to offer people?" he would say. "What is it about me that makes people come to me, talk to me, become friends with me? I have no gifts, no special talents." He undoubtedly had gifts but was not overly conscious of what they might be. What was apparent, though, was that they did not exist for himself: they were to be used for the benefit of others.

Mychal Judge did not tolerate incompetence and became frustrated if trivialities obscured the more obvious and salient priorities of people's lives. Every moment was graced. He wanted to do as much good as he could in the time that was left to him. God was an unconditional lover, not a judge. "This was something he felt deep in the pit of his stomach," said Anthony McNeill. "He was keenly aware of that presence of God's love in the midst of every minute of his life. It was from there that he got his energy, his drive, and his motivation."

He did two hundred push-ups every day and was always pacing rooms. His "power walks" around the city maintained his fitness program. He even went rollerblading in his sixties. He did not like to see any fat on himself and would tell his friends if he suspected they were going over the line. He occasionally trekked for hours out to Coney Island, engaging in conversations with anyone who would speak with him along the way and rewarding himself with a juicy hot dog at journey's end. He enjoyed meeting pals in diners where his huge hands would envelop a mug of coffee as though he were blessing it. If they could get him to sit long enough for a meal, he might choose "a large slice of pie," as he referred to pizza, or food that was ethnically to his taste, such as corned beef and cabbage or Irish stew. He also ordered Asian dishes and could polish off a Chinese meal effortlessly.

His literary diets were also catholic. A daily source of nourishment was a book by Melody Beattie, *The Language of Letting Go*, which is used by members of Alcoholics Anonymous. This through-the-year volume comprises a series of meditations "designed to help you spend a few moments each day remembering what you know." It focuses on the fundamentals of codependency recovery — "letting ourselves feel all our emotions, accepting powerlessness, and owning our own power" and aimed to "help you feel good and assist you in the process of self-care and recovery." The paperback was well thumbed by Father Mychal, who underlined many of its phrases. On the morning of September 11, he would have read an entry entitled, "Conflict and Detachment":

> Today, I will remember that my best relationships have low points. If the low point is the norm, I may want to consider the desirability of the relationship. If the low point is a temporary cycle, I will practice understanding for myself and the other person. God, help me remember that the help and support I want and need does not come in the form of only one person. Help me be open to healthy options for taking care of myself, if my normal support system is not available.

Another form of sustenance was the last meditations of the Jesuit priest Anthony de Mello, who had been director of the Sadhana Institute of Pastoral Counselling in Poona, India. The book was entitled *The Way to Love*. "He had me reading it, other people reading it, the bookstore carrying it, and half of New York leafing it," a friar told me. "He liked its simplicity and the fact that de Mello cut to the quick, connecting the humanity of Christ and the closeness of God to our own experience."

The thoughts, built around short sentences of scripture, embrace such themes as discipleship, going the extra mile, illusion and attachment, as well as the need to love one's enemies. The final entry, on the desire for holiness, which Mychal would have studied, is based on the words: "Therefore you also must be ready; for the Son of Man is coming at an hour you do not expect" (Matt 24:44). It explains that the love of others is not won by the practice of techniques but by being a certain kind of person. The same is true of spirituality, which is neither a commodity to be purchased nor a prize to be gained. What matters is what you are, what you become. Holiness is a grace rather than an achievement, more an awareness than a reward:

Will awareness bring you the holiness you so desire? Yes and no. The fact is you will never know. For true holiness, the type that is not achieved through techniques and efforts and repression, true holiness is completely unself-conscious. You wouldn't have the slightest awareness of its existence in you. Besides you will not care, for even the ambition to be holy will have dropped as you live from moment to moment a life made full and happy and transparent through aware-ness. It is enough for you to be watchful and awake. For in this state your eyes will see the Savior. Nothing else, but absolutely nothing else. Not security, not love, not belong-ing, not beauty, not power, not holiness — nothing else will matter any more.

Judge also valued *The Way of a Pilgrim,* a classic of Ortho-dox spirituality in which an unknown wanderer of the nineteenth century relived a journey through Russia and Siberia, from one holy place to another, in search of the way of prayer. Every day Mychal Judge would repeat the Jesus Prayer: "Lord Jesus Christ, have mercy on me," a meditative rhythm of breathing described in the book.

He was devoted to the Sacred Heart and, above all, to the Virgin Mary. A rosary hung across the steering column in his car. Cruising along in light traffic, he would finger the beads, praying his way through the joyful, sorrowful, and glorious mysteries: "Hail Mary, full of grace, the Lord is with thee. Blessed art thou among women and blessed in the fruit of thy womb, Jesus." In a soft, gravelly voice, he would also bring a favorite prayer to his lips while driving along:

> Our Lady of the Highway
> Be thou our aid setting out
> Our comfort on the way
> Our support in weariness
> Our refuge in danger
> So that under thy guidance

We may in safety reach our destinations
And return unharmed to our homes
Amen.

The writings of the Carmelite nun St. Thérèse of Lisieux, who died in 1897 at the age of twenty-four, also appealed to him, not merely as "the little flower," an image beloved of traditional Catholic piety, but as one who had faced an existential crisis of spiritual darkness, abandonment to God, and the rediscovery of grace *in extremis.* Mychal Judge, who visited the saint's home in northern France, felt she was a contemporary figure in that she had lived under the shadow of death and had been transformed through it. When he realized he was perhaps about to die on September 11, he would probably have been influenced enough by Thérèse of Lisieux to understand that this time of seeming disaster was also a moment of the breaking-in of grace.

He prayed every day to St. Maximilian Kolbe, the Polish Franciscan and founder of the Militia of Mary Immaculate. Kolbe had been imprisoned at the Nazi concentration camp in Auschwitz and, in 1941, had volunteered to take the place of a young father condemned to execution. "His story is absolutely extraordinary," Judge once said. "It is definitely God's grace. The wonderful thing about that is saying yes and accepting that grace. You could say no and walk away. But when we accept it and say yes and go forward, great and wonderful things will happen. It takes courage in the midst of fear, and you do it with the grace of God."

The spirituality of Mychal Judge, then, was an amalgam of the influences that had shaped his life, notably traditional piety and the inspiration of St. Francis. He could stand back from the sentimental aspects of Catholic culture with its dependency on the intercession of the saints and the power of miracles, while at the same time acknowledging this was part of his own spiritual history. But his lived experience introduced him to a deeper revelation of faith. His spiritual maturity was fostered by his discovery of Alcoholics Anonymous, a fellowship for recovering alcoholics.

He carried the A.A. booklet around with him and quoted from it constantly. Some suggested he was more familiar with this text than with certain passages of the Bible.

He displayed an openness to the breadth of spiritual thinking. One of the joys of his later life was a celebration of the fact that, in the Catholic world, traditional spirituality had been set free from some of the confines of scholasticism or traditional Catholic piety. Creation-centered spirituality and liberation theologies spoke increasingly to his own experience. His style of dialoguing with the divine was homely. "We prayed together on several occasions and it was always informal," recalled Stephen Weaver. "He would never read from a book. He would always speak spontaneously and in a conversational manner. He talked to Jesus with a sort of litany of praise. 'Well, Lord, we just wanna thank and praise you. You're very good. You've given us a wonderful day and allowed us to meet some wonderful people. And we thank you for Joe, who lost his wife, and we thank you for Mary, who is not very well right now. We ask you, Lord, to keep all of them in your care.'"

It was a review of the day, informing Jesus of all his adventures and asking him to shed the light of his compassion and grace on what had happened. The spontaneous office would always include a personal postscript: "I thank you, Lord. Just help me to stay sober — to stay loving you and serving you."

4

SHADOWS OF THE SELF

⊶∞⊷

MYCHAL JUDGE was never a theological sophisticate. He passed through the motions of his theological training without essentially taking on board a method. At times people found him anti-intellectual, but, as the years went on, his theology became grounded in the human experience of being a Franciscan priest in love with life — but aware of his own wounds.

Stephen Weaver explained that Father Mychal's theology was of a practical nature. Traditional theological argument frustrated him because it was a contemporary equivalent of disputing the number of angels on the head of a pin. Far more urgent questions were how he was going to relate to people on the streets or help people with HIV/AIDS. His was a comprehensive theological stance embracing the fullness of humanity. According to Weaver:

> It would probably have surprised Mychal to be informed that his theology had much in common with Pope John Paul II. The papal notion of what it is to be fully human was very close to Mychal's own heart, even though he might not have been able to articulate it. Mychal was of the school that acknowledged that the perfect human was Christ in the fullness of his incarnation. He honored Christ's embrace of human suffering and death, and the transformation of that through the resurrection. Mychal gloried in his own humanity and found in that a fellow feeling with the person of Jesus. That is what he brought to bear in his ministry.

While Mychal Judge never tired of Franciscan life, he adored his family. "If the friary should catch fire," he would say, "I would take two things out with me: my Franciscan habit and the pictures of my sisters." When Richard Rohr visited the friary, he was struck by the smallness and simplicity of Mychal's room:

> He had a few posters on the wall of some artistic merit, but the rest was clean and simple. I always wished I had as little junk as he had. He must have taken his poverty rather seriously. I did not sense he was a guy who was ambitious for fancy things or a collector. He was a poor man in that sense. His smile came very naturally, not only his ability to smile at himself and make fun of himself, but to laugh at some of the mistakes of the order and of the church — and some of their pretentiousness. He did not get angry. He just smiled at it. That was very Franciscan.

Brian Carroll, a psychotherapist and psychoanalyst, thought Mychal epitomized the words of St. Irenaeus of Lyons: "The splendor of God is the human being fully realized." To be fully human was to be fully alive. Anyone who ever experienced a service he conducted or heard him preach saw this aliveness and humanity in unambiguous mode. He could turn a church into a small chapel or a cathedral into the most intimate country church. He walked outside the sanctuary among the people. Carroll commented:

> He could see your eyes, hear your groaning, notice people looking at their watches, or twisting their wedding band with ambivalence. He was sensitive to the movements of people. What allowed him to be so sensitive was the sensitivity in his own life. The greatest gift he gave to me and a number of other friars was teaching by example how to break out of the box, the corporate lingo, the sanctuary, and to go down among people. When you start preaching or ministering down in the front pew, you are taking a great risk because you are getting really close. You are seeing and hearing them. You have to think on your feet. You also have to *feel*, so you are going to be surprised by what you say.

The Catholic writer Flannery O'Connor's description of art as "a house waiting to be haunted" could be applied to Mychal Judge, who was "scared to death" when he stepped out to preach because he did not know what he was going to say. At the end of the homily, the congregation might indeed have been surprised by what they had heard and seen. But they would have loved it. Yet the most surprised of anyone would have been Mychal himself. Brian Carroll told me his sermons were homilies waiting to be haunted:

> It was his love of God and his love of humanity which made him a friar. He put humanity and God together. He was able to synthesize that. It came out in his preaching. He haunted his humanity with God. He did that in an incredibly beautiful and simple way. I think he brought that same spirit to everybody he met. You hear stories constantly of strangers he met on the street feeling touched by him. That haunting spirit of God permeated everything he did.

MYCHAL JUDGE was six feet one inch tall and weighed around 180 pounds. He was lean and muscular, with piercing hazel-blue eyes and big, strong Celtic hands. "I know he was an American but there was definitely a Celtic personality in there," Father Anthony McNeill observed. Meticulous in appearance, he believed people should always look smart: "Comb your hair and polish your shoes," he would say, "because you want to look your best. And always use your height because you want to present yourself as a strong presence."

With the looks of a matinee idol, he had great photogenic appeal — with more than a touch of vanity when it came to having his picture taken. The dashing fire chaplain was even known to spray his hair before leaving on an emergency call and at other times to double-check in store window panes that his high standards had not been assaulted by an unexpected gust of wind. "I'm not so sure if he hadn't had his nails done too somewhere along the line," quipped raconteur Malachy McCourt.

Whether breakfasting with the Clintons, shaking hands with the mayor, or acting as guide of souls to members of the New York press club, he liked to be in lens-shot, if possible alongside a celebrity. When Jacqueline Kennedy was being honored by an arts society, of which he was a member, he urged a Franciscan friend: "Come on, let's meet Jackie." He was always eager to see his picture in the papers. Friends would be sent copies of articles with the coverage he had received ringed in black ink. Publicity seemed to follow him around like a newshound. But he also had the courage to appear at events where the camera's eye might expose his involvement with controversial causes.

The ever ebullient Mychal Judge loved the image he had cultivated, but partly in the Franciscan sense of knowing that it reflected the beauty of God. He had been blessed with good looks and could pose in the style of a Hollywood star or a debonair politician. But in all this there was something beyond mere narcissism. It was essentially a way of promoting a peculiarly Franciscan earthiness and showing it to be part of the revelation of God's beauty and truth. There were also more pragmatic considerations. His church held an annual collection for the poor, St. Anthony's Bread, when thousands of dollars would be raised. One year the money was stolen the same day. The incident received extensive press coverage. Many New Yorkers were incensed because the poor had lost out. It was Father Mychal who engineered the media campaign to bring the felony to public attention and ensure that a vast amount of money was collected in response. At the same time, however, he made certain that news camera operators captured his image alongside those of the police chief in drawing people back into what was essentially an act of giving to those who were most in need. This was characteristic of his ability to manipulate the tools of the trade in a positive way. But he was never manipulative in a devious sense. PR even gave him some serenity and comfort. Carroll considered him an adept politician, publicist, and communicator schooled in the American art of using human drama to draw people into issues of concern and a New

York penchant for "giving that a whole patina of street wisdom and a certain amount of scintillation, titillation even." The skills came naturally to the man "as much a New Yorker as any of the powerful figures associated with the city who have done similar things for more secular ends."

The smile in the pictures was always natural, yet many New Yorkers reading about him in their daily newspapers would have been unaware of the personal hurdles he had striven hard to overcome. Richard Rohr noticed his genuine love of people was complemented by a self-deprecating humility and an ability to laugh at his own failures. He was never pretentious and could admit his shadow side — "not in a put-down way but one which said, 'Yeah, isn't that *me?*'" Rohr pointed out that, like many people, Mychal knew his motivations were mixed and not always pure. He would say, "I'm doing it for me too, and I'm getting plenty out of this."

He also noted that Mychal had suave expertise in knowing how to grease the wheels of the system and make it work for him. He could move inside institutions. He got mileage out of his perks in entertaining others but never lost sight of the fact that life was provisional. One day Mychal took him on a tour of New York and pulled up on Fifth Avenue in his fire car right in front of St. Patrick's Cathedral. Rohr spluttered: "You're not going to leave it there?" He replied: "Oh, yes. No one will touch it." and went on to give Rohr a forty-five-minute tour of the building. "He never made any pretense of being a saint, which in some ways made him such a believable holy man. He had a good, honest self-acceptance."

But Mychal Judge was particularly hurt by the fact that he never knew his father, and this troubled him throughout his life. Yet, paradoxically, his paternal qualities seemed ingrained. "He was steady, thoughtful, wise, regal, warm, compassionate, and completely understanding," observed Brian Carroll. "He was the father every man wanted, and I think he was the father he had wanted."

Father Anthony McNeill said it was clear that Mychal regretted not having someone to guide him when he was younger, a father-type figure who could take him under his wing and give him direction. He also wished he had done further studies and earned a master's degree. It created a determination to seize the day because opportunities tended not to pass twice. His intellectual shortcomings resulted in a certain inferiority complex. He longed to be more academic, yet was never motivated to study.

He also suffered from what he called "that Irish guilt." He felt he could always be "working harder for the Lord." When his answering machine was full of messages, he would be racked with anxiety over whether he could possibly meet all the needs. When the machine wasn't full, he would start to worry that he wasn't needed. He tried to be all things for all people. He was a modest man, but he knew also he had something to offer and share. Brian Carroll said Father Mychal believed he had been given a great gift. God loved him and he loved God:

> I don't think he trusted anyone else with preaching that word when he could do it. It was not that he would do it better, but he sensed that he had a special relationship with God. He wasn't going to entrust it to someone else. I think he knew that, through his own pain, his own suffering, his own anxiety, his own love, and his own journey, he could relate to people in an intimate way. It wasn't a self-gloating. There was a humility about it but also an awareness that he knew he had something special. It was almost paradoxical. He was one of the most humble men I ever met and one of the men most tormented with anxiety I ever met professionally or in my personal life. At the same time he was one of the most confident men I ever met.

A one-time heavy drinker who even had blackouts, Mychal Judge found the courage to confront his own addiction. His involvement with Alcoholics Anonymous comprised a systematic, long-term program of recovery in which he was able to blend his Franciscan commitment to the poor with a more profound spirituality of honesty, openness, and willingness. It created an inner freedom to explore his own humanity and to feel comfortable, not only in being among other alcoholics, but precisely in expressing who he was with them as he listened to their stories and shared his own. "I think he knew he was a broken person who had been healed and put together again," said Father Anthony McNeill. "He felt he was graced and depended on God for his sobriety. While aware of this brokenness, he knew also that he had an ability to touch people, to make sense of life for people and stand alongside them as they were struggling. That was his self-awareness. God was his Savior who had managed to get his life together again after his alcoholism. It was something he felt every minute of the day."

Mychal Judge embodied the spirit of Thornton Wilder's maxim that in God's army only the wounded may serve. He carried around two quotations that were placed back to back in a laminated wallet. On one side were words from the French Dominican Henri Lacordaire's "Thou Art a Priest Forever":

> To live in the midst of the world without wishing its pleasures; to be a member of each family, yet belonging to none; to share all sufferings; to penetrate all secrets; to heal all wounds; to go from men to God and offer him their prayers; to return from God to men to bring pardon and hope; to have a heart of fire for charity and a heart of bronze for chastity; to teach and to pardon, console and bless always — what a glorious life! And it is yours, O priest of Jesus Christ!

On the other side was a quotation from page 449 of the "Big Book" of Alcoholics Anonymous:

> Acceptance is the answer to *all* my problems today. When I am disturbed it is because I find some person, place, thing, or situation — some fact of my life — unacceptable to me,

and I can find no serenity, until I accept that person, place, thing, or situation as being exactly the way it is supposed to be at this moment. Nothing, absolutely nothing happens in God's world by mistake. Until I could accept my alcoholism, I could not stay sober; unless I accept life completely on life's terms, I cannot be happy. I need to concentrate not so much on what needs to be changed in the world as on what needs to be changed in me and in my attitudes.

A.A. seems to have been the catalyst that enabled him to accept himself as a holy man — and a recovering alcoholic. More-over, it effected the process of coming to terms with his sexual orientation as he made the journey from an awareness of same-sex attraction as pathology toward the integration of his sexuality as part of his personal identity. Like many Catholics in his situa-tion, he struggled to emerge from a climate that discouraged an easy acceptance of homosexuality into the challenge of coming out as a gay man who also happened to be a priest.

As he began to own his sexuality, he found he was able to min-ister more effectively to others. In particular, he could share the experiences of gay people with understanding and authenticity. This sense of self-availability was never more in evidence than at the height of the AIDS pandemic when he told dying young men that he understood their pain because he too was gay. In other circles, he had to walk the line of being God's servant and shep-herd of people and at the same time hold back his true identity because of a fear of personal rejection.

The nature of Mychal Judge's sexuality was revealed by gay activists shortly after his death and has since been well aired in the media. Many considered such disclosure a hasty and insen-sitive intrusion at a time of personal and national grief. Some friends vehemently denied the priest had been gay. Others feared the truth of his life would overshadow the heroism of his death and sour the fruits of his ministry. Paradoxically a gulf grew between some of the very people Mychal Judge had once managed to unite.

But the priest had already divulged to a number of straight and gay friends in America and Britain that he was homosexual; moreover, he had told them that, when it came to writing his autobiography, this dimension of his life would not be excluded or glossed over. The dilemma added to the emotional strain he felt at times but, for all this, Mychal Judge was never pathologically lonely or tormented, which is not to suggest that he did not have his darker periods.

The bad memories of childhood, innate feelings of self-doubt, and a lingering sense of Irish guilt (which might have propelled him to work far beyond the call of duty) created their own spells of anxiety and depression. But, through it all, Father Judge came closer, not only to God, but also to the hearts of his beloved New Yorkers, whose lives were deepened and transformed by his presence. It was a vocation for creating a spiritual landscape out of broken land.

Part Two

GOD'S MINSTREL

What are God's servants but his minstrels, who must inspire
the hearts of men and stir them to spiritual joy.

— The Early Companions of St. Francis,
Mirror of Perfection, 100

5

BROKEN LAND

All that I dig with the spade
I do it with my Father's aid

All that I dig with the spade
I do it with my Saviour's aid

All that I dig with the spade
I do it with the Spirit's aid

All that I dig with the spade
I do it in God the Three's aid
Each turning of the soil I make
I do it for the Three in One's sake.

— "Breaking New Land"
by David Adam

Mychal Judge's ancestors lived in a country that had been shaped by the spirituality of the Celts, a landscape where divine glory was interwoven into the ordinary patterns of everyday life. Celtic poetry exuded the force and beauty of nature and foreshadowed Franciscan writing in honoring sun and moon, sea and earth. The family roots lay in what many regarded as the poorest county in Ireland — and the prettiest. Lush countryside — mountains, lakes, rivers, pastures, and boglands — formed the texture of Mychal Judge's Gaelic heritage. County Leitrim, in the north of Eire, gained its name from the Irish word *Liathdroim,* meaning "the gray hill ridge." In the past, many of its hills had been coal and iron ore mines, owing to the large deposits of minerals from the River Shannon. Measuring fifty-two miles by sixteen miles, it had the shortest shoreline in the country. The surfaces were extremely uneven but the landscapes stunning. Glencar Waterfall inspired the poet W. B. Yeats.

Here farmers carried on the traditions of past centuries. Mychal's father, Michael Judge, was of farming stock. Born and raised in the scenic lakeside village of Keshcarrigan near Carrick-on-Shannon, he had grown up on a small farm. John Keaney, who now owns the land, told me how he had first met Father Mychal when he came to visit the village in the 1980s. Mychal learned how his father had sold his twenty-eight acres alongside the lake, which was purchased by Mr. Keaney's father in the 1960s for a mere £300. In March 2000 Father Mychal returned with his nephew, Michael, and visited his father's birthplace. John Keaney and his wife, Christina, showed them what was left of the old house — part of a stone gable wall which formed part of a cattle shed. "He was really delighted," said John Keaney. "He took a pebble out of the wall and took it back to America as a souvenir. He said that, had he won the Lotto, he would not have been as happy. He could not believe it."

John Keaney remembered being struck by Father Judge's presence. "There was something in him. Some kind of treasure." Writing to him after that visit, Father Mychal had commented: "For a long time to come young Michael and I will remember the very warm welcome you extended to us in your lovely home. It was the highlight of the day's trip to the Emerald Isle.... I was thrilled, John, that you took us up the path and showed me the spot where my father's home sat. I was there two or three times before but never so far in the land.... Good feelings. Will now have a blessed spring and summer. You have my prayers."

Mychal Judge's mother, Mary Fallon, came from Creevylea near Drumkeerin. Intriguingly, just a few miles away lay Creevelea, home of the last Franciscan friary to be founded in Ireland before the suppression of the monasteries in the sixteenth century. In the center of the north side of the irregularly shaped cloister were a number of pillars with carvings. One showed St. Francis receiving the stigmata.

Ancestors of the Australian prime ministers Stanley Melbourne Bruce and Francis Forde hailed from Leitrim, as did John Harte, the premier of British Columbia, and Robert Strawbridge, the man who brought Methodism to the United States.

The Great Famine of the mid-nineteenth century had a devastating effect on Leitrim, resulting in an exodus principally to the east coast of the United States. America's first tidal wave of immigration from Ireland coincided with the construction of the Erie Canal, an artificial waterway in upstate New York, the longest canal in the world. The nation's "gold cord" converted New York City into a metropolis and guaranteed its place as the country's most influential port. Former small farmers from Ireland provided much of the manpower, sweating their way through woods, rocky barrens, and mosquito-infested swamps to complete the project. Many died. Despite their contribution to America's future, the "bogtrotters" prompted taunts from New Yorkers about their uncouth appearance. On the eve of St. Patrick's Day, the natives would indulge in the art of "paddy-making," stuffing a dummy with rags, smearing molasses on its painted face, stringing potatoes and codfish around its neck, and resting a bottle of whiskey in its pocket.

Many Irish immigrants settled in Brooklyn, one of five New York City boroughs created from the amalgamation of hamlets, villages, towns, and cities. The Dutch had settled on the western part of Long Island. The village of Breukelen, meaning "broken land," was once inhabited by an Indian subtribe called the Canarsie. It was granted a municipal form of government in 1646. The name evolved from Breukelen to Brockland to Bricklin to Brookline and finally to Brooklyn. Residents were said to prefer its slower pace to the tempo of Manhattan.

At the turn of the century, a fifth of American's new immigrants were Irish. Although natives of Leitrim, Michael Judge and Mary Fallon met for the first time on a ship heading across the Atlantic in the 1920s. Like many others who left Ireland, they came in search of new life and opportunities. They, too, set up home in Brooklyn.

Father Mychal was always proud of the fact that his parents had been immigrants and had carved out a new life for themselves. For him, they were personifications of the American dream. He would gaze at the Statue of Liberty and wonder at the feelings of joy and hope that his brave parents had experienced as their boat came into New York harbor. They had no idea of the blessings and sorrows that would lie ahead but they trusted that the God who had brought them to the shores would continue to care for them. Mychal Judge's friend Tom Ferriter, whose mother also came from Leitrim, recalled Mychal talking about the hardships his parents had faced: "They had grown up so poor. When they got to America they luxuriated in their new life but were terrified someone would take it from them."

Mychal Judge was born in Brooklyn, on May 11, 1933. He was the first of twins — Dympna arrived two days later. They had an elder sister, Erin. A close bond developed among all three. Mychal was baptized Robert Emmett Judge in St. Paul's Church, Brooklyn, on June 4, 1933, by Father John Donlon. (The name Mychal would come later.) His early education was at St. Paul's Elementary School. Like other boys of his time, he spent his young days playing stickball and riding his bike. But childhood pleasures were soon marred by tragedy. His father was taken ill and spent more than three years in the hospital. In failing health, he was always concerned about his children who were not allowed into the hospital to see him. They could only wave to their father through a window.

Mr. Judge's death, when Mychal was just six, had a devastating effect. "I never called anyone 'Dad,'" he would later lament. "I've always been very much on my own." Mr. Judge had run Butler's grocery store in Brooklyn, and years later Mychal discovered that a fellow friar was the son of a truck driver who used to deliver food to the shop. He once had the opportunity to ask the man what his father had been like: "Open that door," he said, "and you'll find a full-length mirror on the back. Look in the mirror and what you see is your father."

As a young immigrant widow, Mrs. Judge had to seek other means of making ends meet. She rented rooms to young transients, who would stay for three to six months. Responsibilities fell heavily on young Mychal, who had to assume the male role, undertaking repair work around the house. Every time a tenant or boarder moved out, Mychal and his sisters would have to paint the room. Mychal also had to help with the laundry.

With the family short of money, he would run errands and do odd jobs, such as cleaning people's windows on Dean Street, where they lived. He even packed up rags and cycled over to Manhattan to shine shoes in front of the Flatiron Building, Grand Central Station, and Penn Station. "Although we had nothing," he once said, "my mother made us feel like we were upper middle class."

Committing himself later to a life of poverty did not come as a shock because he had known it materially and emotionally from an early age. One friend, Michael Mulligan, explained: "The poorer you were or the more impoverished you were, the more he loved you. He had lived poverty as a child and understood its shortcomings. He empathized with the shame of poverty. He knew what it was like not to have a new baseball glove or a pair of shoes. I saw that in him. Mychal knew that poverty, that hell, both as a kid and as a grown man."

One of Mychal Judge's Irish friends in New York, Brendan Fay, pointed out that his father's illness and death had affected his life so much that he was still talking about it into his sixties: "He wished he could have had the experience of having a father like so many others. There was a deep sense of loss and of longing for a real experience of a father in his life. The only memories he had were of his father being ill."

Mychal regretted not having had a father to support him in the preteen days, teen years, and early adolescence. For example, playing catch was a rite of passage in America. The father taught the son how to throw a baseball and how to catch it with a glove.

Mychal missed out on that. As a lad he did not have the vocabulary to articulate how he felt. He wasn't able to be analytical about what had happened. The pain was real but the sense of loss was repressed.

"He told me over and over again how much he missed having a father," said Brian Carroll. "He remembered his mother going to the hospital every day to see him. In order to understand Mychal Judge, I think you have to understand that he was a man who believed he had lost something in not having a father with him into his adulthood. He compensated for that by fathering other people. He had a very fatherly way about him. His father must have had an influence on him early in life — he must have been a wonderful man."

Father Mychal would often discuss the absence of his father with Richard Rohr, who had researched the psychological implications of "the father wound" and spoken publicly about it. Through his work, Rohr experienced how many young men, in particular, desired surrogate fathers and mentors. Even some "gender identity confusion" in young men, he discovered, was not constitutional homosexuality, but simply "father hunger." The more Rohr traveled to different cultures, the more he felt this "father wound" was "perhaps the most universal wound on this earth." So many men, often by reason of military service, death, or employment, had not been seriously involved in the upbringing of their sons and daughters. As a result, there had been huge anger, mistrust, fear, and also "desire" toward men, particularly men in authority. Mychal Judge was fascinated by Rohr's findings and listened to his tapes. "Almost every time we were together he would bring up the loss of his father," said Rohr, author of *The Wild Man's Journey*:

> It must have been a very real wound in his life. He did not know his father at all. Yet he basically communicated a very healthy, likeable, and trustworthy manhood to other men, often men who did not know their fathers at all or were so insecure in that area. They were men so doubting

of their own fatherhood and manhood. Somehow he seems to have come to it in his own unique way. I don't think you would call him a person of great intellectual authority or inner authority in terms of wisdom, but he had a kind of personal authority in knowing people. That was where he earned his fatherhood. I had done a lot of work with men's spirituality, and he talked about his own somewhat weak relationship with his father, as he saw it. He wondered if that wasn't what had given him a compassion for other men. He saw his own wounds and seemed to be in touch with them and not embarrassed by them.

Rohr thinks that, through his work with other people, especially the firefighters, Judge was undoubtedly trying to fill some of the paternal gap he felt in his own upbringing. He regarded him as a "classic example" of a wounded healer, who used his wound, not as something to whine about or to blame others for, but as the occasion for his own transformation in God the Father. Judge even talked to Rohr about fatherhood as they drove around that day on June 2001, but no longer needed to psychoanalyze it. "In that regard, he was similar to Henri Nouwen, but also less tortured than Henri. Mychal was a simple man, in the best sense of that term. Henri was complex."

Mychal Judge went through all of the rites of passage of a Catholic boy growing up in Brooklyn and was confirmed shortly after his tenth birthday. He had a natural faith and was grateful for what his mother and sisters had passed on to him. There were devotions, missions, and retreats in a once self-contained Catholic culture since dissipated by the pressures of modern life and society. He would often look back with a wry bemusement in the way in which he had been a child of his time. He was reared in an era when deference to church leadership was more marked. It was a church in which everyone had a place in a hierarchical order and, for a young man, perhaps seeking out a greater sense of familial warmth than he had experienced at home, there was something inherently attractive in it. Various priests from his childhood were heroic figures, some of them Franciscans, and he wanted to emulate them.

Stephen Weaver sensed that, locked deep inside Mychal Judge, were two characters: an insecure boy and a more hopeful young man who had left his family in Brooklyn to begin his engagement with the wider world:

> I think he felt ambivalently about the family. He could some-times speak quite harshly of his mother, her own struggles and the expectations she placed on him. She put demands on him to perform, to be a good boy, to make her proud of him. She cast a long shadow over the struggles he had to face to become his own person.

Mychal Judge's relationship with his mother might, to some extent, have influenced the complex way he related to the fig-ure of Mary. He had inherited from Catholic piety a devotion to "The Blessed Mother," as Mary is often addressed in American Catholicism. But he had to filter this through his experience of his own mother, which was not always as blessed as it might have been. Weaver often had the sense he was less confident about speaking of the feminine aspect of God than he was of the mas-culine. Nonetheless his manifest compassion, capacity to nurture, and recognition of how healing intimate relationships could be indicated that his feminine side was well integrated in the sec-ond half of his life. This was in part a reflection of his coming to terms with his own sexuality and opening out to the experience of intimacy.

It was not until his mother's death in the 1970s that he felt released into a much more humane and rounded relationship with Mother Church. He never ceased to love either his mother or indeed the Roman Catholic Church, but, like any good rela-tionship with parents, these relationships went through significant phases of development.

Father Patrick Fitzgerald stressed that Mrs. Judge, a fine singer, had been "a very responsible person," who carried the personal burden of living in the late 1930s, when the United States was coming out of the Depression. She provided for her three children and wanted them to be college educated. Her dreams had revolved around education. She did not have any money, but she worked hard so they might be college educated. Both girls graduated from a private and prestigious Catholic women's college, and Mychal went to a seminary. It was a great achievement.

Mychal Judge's friend Manhattan businessman Frank Murphy, senior vice-president of basketball affairs for the New York Knickerbockers and New York Liberty, was also the son of Irish immigrants from Brooklyn. "We were fed and clothed but we had very simple parents," he said. "We both went to work very early. We had the Irish ethic, peculiar to New York and to the part of Brooklyn we were from, of very strong traditions, belief in respecting authority, a strong relationship with the church, and that dear old Catholic secrecy. 'What'll the neighbors say? Never let anybody know anything bad that's going on.'"

Murphy revealed that this secrecy had featured in their last telephone conversation the Friday before September 11:

> The great part of the conversation, probably for the thousandth time, was the effect of such secrecy and how you deal with the Irish Catholic guilt that we grew up with. It was all about the need for perfection. You had to be perfect. You could never do anything wrong because that would be a reflection on you and your family. Mychal was almost two different people: the outside person that he most certainly was in his ability to deal with people and to speak publicly, and then this other person who had fears and anxieties that the average man or woman he met would never know about.

Mychal Judge would often joke about Irish guilt with Brendan Fay: "Oh, my God," he would say, "the guilt, the guilt, the guilt." Fay said that, growing up in a household where the needs were so great, Father Mychal perhaps never reached the point where he could say: "I have done it. I have accomplished it. I have met these needs." He could never fully satisfy his mother or the situation in which he found himself.

New York state senator Tom Duane also detected guilt in Father Mychal. He, too, believed he was more complicated than he appeared. Accompanying the good works was a deep-rooted streak of self-doubt, tamed by humor:

> If you are Irish and you're a Catholic, you are going to have guilt about something, whether it is deserved or not. His life was very much about service to other people and bringing God to them. But he also had an inner life that questioned how he was living his life. I remember talking to him once in Greenwich Village. When I saw him next, he said: "Gee, I hope I didn't insult you or that I was too flip with what I said to you when we met a couple of weeks ago." I hadn't remembered him saying anything that had been mean or sarcastic. It made me realize that he questioned himself, that he had human feelings and that he didn't think of himself as being perfect.

6

THE TRAIN TO CALLICOON

———⚬⊗⚬———

I T WAS DURING Mychal Judge's shoe-shining excursions to Penn
Station that he discovered the nearby Church of St. Francis of
Assisi. While the leather sandals of the friars would never benefit
from his polishing prowess, he found himself drawn to their lifestyle. "Where else in the world would you go?" he once said. "I
remember the lower church and the fountain and a friar. I loved
him and his brown robes. I used to follow him around everywhere.
I knew then that I wanted to be a friar. I realized that I didn't care
for material things all that much." But the call to religious life was
matched by another strong conviction: "I felt a tremendous urge
to be a priest and answered yes."

Mychal, who was still in seventh grade at St. Paul's, Brooklyn,
struck up conversations with the friar, who had an equally outgoing personality. The boy may even have looked up to him as
a father figure. Through the meetings, Mychal discerned a vocation to Franciscan priesthood. While at St. Francis's Preparatory
School in Brooklyn, he successfully applied for seminary training. He transferred to St. Joseph's Seraphic Seminary, Callicoon,
New York, 129 miles northwest of New York City, high above
the Delaware River valley, on the Pennsylvania–New York State
border.

Jim O'Donnell, who traveled there by train with the teenaged
Mychal in 1948, recollected the journey: "The train was packed
with seminarians and there was a lot of anticipation. We all had
black suits on and black ties, and some of us got drinks from the
bar. By the time we reached Callicoon it was evening, but one
of the friars was there to greet us. All of our stuff got thrown in

a truck, but we had to walk up the hill, which took about ten or fifteen minutes. We went into a basement room, where they served us cold cuts. The best thing about Callicoon was that the brothers made the bread."

The seminary was a large, gray stone building. Two overcrowded dormitories on the top floor — one for seniors, the other for juniors — housed 140 young men. Each student had a bed, a chair, and half a locker, but they had to take a bucket to a tub of hot water so they could wash in their own sinks. Morning prayers, Mass, and breakfast were followed by bed-making and room-cleaning. Classes sandwiched lunch but between 3:00 P.M. and 5:30 P.M. there was recreation. The students had a half-day off every Wednesday and Saturday and would go for walks in the surrounding countryside.

Jim O'Donnell recalled that Mychal had to struggle, not only with his academic work but also a stutter, which was corrected during speech therapy sessions back in New York during the holidays. He was an excited, outgoing teenager, who laughed a lot and seemed to fit in. He worked hard but when it came to exams found the absorption of facts eluding him. He would have to repeat phrases to himself over and over again. His stronger gift was for remembering people. His strong presence veered toward extroversion more than introversion. Fellow students saw him as an ordinary seminarian, who was "goal-oriented" in that he had a strong desire to be a priest.

Judge once told a journalist that the seminarians had been "locked in for a year and a day" with no radio, television, telephone, newspapers, or even talking allowed, except for one hour daily. Families could visit only four times a year for four hours. The days had been filled with prayer, study of Catholic tradition, and the rule of the order. "God gave me the vocation, considering my person, to be a follower of St. Francis, where I truly believe I fit perfectly. I would never want to be anything else."

Father Patrick Fitzgerald met Mychal at Callicoon — fifty years to the day before the World Trade Center attacks. The semester usually began on September 8 on the feast of the birthday of the Blessed Virgin Mary, but in 1951 it was delayed until September 11: "To be a Franciscan brother was not his calling. He was called to be a Franciscan priest. Not a Jesuit. Not a Dominican. Not a diocesan but a Franciscan priest — the two were welded together."

It was recommended at one stage that Mychal Judge be dismissed from the seminary because a standard personality test suggested he was an unsuitable candidate for the priesthood. Recognizing Mychal's gifts, the guardian refused to accept the interpretation given by the assessor. But it wasn't only Mychal's spiritual identity that was under formation at Callicoon. His penchant for publicity was also taking shape. On one occasion Archbishop Fulton J. Sheen, Catholic superstar of American TV, was giving a lecture at a nearby university. The seminarians dutifully attended and listened intently to the priest dubbed "The Microphone of God" because of his powers of communication. But Mychal Judge went a step further: he succeeded in getting his picture taken with Archbishop Sheen. Friends were never able to fathom how he managed to pull it off, but these were clearly signs that the star-struck teenager would not be fighting shy of the limelight as his own priesthood unfolded.

Those days, though, were still far off. During the summer holidays, the seminarian had to take what work he could find, including loading trucks, to earn money. Times were still hard for the family, but his mother and sisters came to visit him in the seminary. Mrs. Judge was an entertaining woman with a strong Irish accent and a great sense of humor. She always drew a crowd. The seminary had not been designed for women visitors. Once she ended up in the men's room on the first floor. Rejoining the group in a visiting parlor, she quipped: "Oh, they have the prettiest sinks in there."

Stephen Weaver found Mychal's stories about his Franciscan training harrowing. Mychal was the most warm and affectionate human being, but he had embraced the rigor of the preconciliar model of formation, untouched by the human sciences and psychological insights, like a hairshirt he had to wear close to his skin. It would always irritate and prevent him from being "truly real and present." At the same time it helped him appreciate the image of Francis embracing the figure of Christ on the cross, and he strove to reproduce it in his own life. He pursued the novitiate life dutifully and saw its disciplines as a necessary function of his formation. He was expected to suffer and to know privation. But it took its toll in human terms. He was often lonely and isolated in the course of his training. He recognized that he had sublimated a lot of his own desire to show affection toward the people he loved: "I am sure this manifested itself later. I have the strong impression he was something of a shadow of his *later* self in his younger days. The photographs show a thinner, leaner, and sadder figure."

It is therefore not surprising to learn that the origins of his alcoholism could be traced to those days. He was one of a number of seminarians who would sneak into the sacristy and swig from the reserves of unconsecrated communion wine. A fellow student confirmed:

> His drinking began in the seminary. He would take a little nip of altar wine — nothing in any great quantity. For seminarians who knew they were addicted, this was a way in which they could satisfy their craving. A little alcohol would do it. They knew they couldn't get a bottle and get drunk or they would be thrown out.

After Callicoon, Mychal Judge spent a year at what was then known as St. Bonaventure Monastery, the novitiate in Paterson, New Jersey, where he was received into the Franciscan order on August 12, 1954, by Father Cassian Kirk, the Callicoon rector. He was twenty-one and took the name "Fallon Michael." In those days men and women joining religious communities were required to change their baptismal names to denote their entry into a new way of life. So Robert Emmett Judge decided to opt for an amalgam of his parents' names. When members of orders were permitted return to their baptismal names after the Second Vatican Council, he retained "Michael" as his first name and "Fallon" as his second name. In later years he proudly coined the name "Mychal" (his own spelling) to differentiate it from the other Michaels on the list of sacramental duties in the community.

His first vows were taken at Paterson in August 1955 before Father Donald Hoag, the head of Holy Name Province at that time. Between 1955 and 1957, he undertook philosophical studies at St. Francis College, Rye Beach, New Hampshire. In addition to their academic work, the students were assigned to various work crews. Judge was selected for the paint group but, because of the rooms he had had to decorate at home as a boy, he resented what he was expected to do. A fellow seminarian recalled: "Just to look at a paintbrush made him anxious, but in those days we were afraid to manifest our true feelings. All he could do was give some family background to the superior and ask if there was another job he could take." Like his classmates, he was awarded a bachelor of arts degree from St. Bonaventure University, but it was not then the custom for seminarians to take part in the graduation ceremony.

In 1957 Mychal Judge began his four-year theology course at Holy Name College, Washington, D.C. Father Francis Muller, who taught canon law and moral and pastoral theology, offered this assessment: "He was well behaved. He never gave any trouble. He was never under suspicion for anything. But he wasn't brilliant academically. He didn't know canon law by heart like some of them. He was a good student, though, and passed all his exams. He told me later he had been an alcoholic there. I said I had never seen him drunk. He said he had made sure of that."

On August 20, 1958, he made his final profession before Father Celsus Wheeler, the provincial, at Christ the King Seminary, Allegany, New York. That day had been the memorial of St. Bernard of Clairvaux, the French abbot and doctor of the church who had entered the Cistercian order when he too was in his twenties.

Father Edward Flanagan, O.F.M., recalled a summer school in 1960 at St. Bonaventure University, eighty miles south of Buffalo.

Flanagan was about to enter his first year of theological studies in Washington, Judge his fourth. He met Mychal as part of a class of young men who were entering their final year of theology in preparation for ordination to the priesthood:

> They included some very dynamic personalities and were very good role models for the first-year theologians. They were very outgoing and talented people. Mike was one of those in a special way. He had a very transparent personality. He was open and he laughed easily. He saw the irony in some human situations even then. Mike was quick to pick up the idiosyncrasies of the professors. He could imitate mannerisms and laugh about them, but always in good fun. He was never unkind and uncharitable. He was perceptive even in his twenties and very understanding of human life. He was a good person to be around in our recreation room because he would laugh. It came, however, from a reservoir of a serious approach toward life. As a student he was solid. I don't think he was above average in his class. I was struck by a very human presence, and in that humanity there was a spirituality. He had a conviction about what he was about and why he was doing it.

Mychal Judge was ordained deacon on the eve of the feast of Saint Michael, in September 1960. The apostolic delegate, Archbishop (later Cardinal) Egidio Vagnozzi ordained him a priest on February 25, 1961, in Mount St. Sepulchre Shrine at the Franciscan Monastery in Washington, D.C. It was a cold, rainy day. Mychal never forgot how hands had been laid firmly on his head and he had been "gifted with priesthood." It was a "glorious" moment, but he later commented that he had had no inkling of what lay ahead: "I knew I would say Mass and preach, that I would baptize, bury the dead, and perform weddings. The rest was all in the hands of God. I could never have dreamt of all the parish years I would enjoy."

His ordination card included two prayers: "May the name of my father, Michael, be written in Your Sacred Heart, O Jesus," and "I give thanks to my Lord Jesus Christ for my mother, sisters, relatives, teachers and friends, through whose prayers and sacrifices He has deigned to share with me His Priesthood." He felt ready and keen to commence his ministry. But at the same time there was also a sense that being a good priest would mean not only being faithful to God but also fulfilling the hopes that he imagined his family had placed in him. This inevitably created a burden of duty and expectation that he felt he had to live up to.

He also felt ashamed of what he considered to be his own poor educational record. Theology and philosophy had been assault courses in academic fitness that he simply had to endure and survive. The way the subjects had been taught in the scholastic system had not given him opportunities to explore the field in more enterprising ways. His sense of leadership emerged through his living the Franciscan charism of joy and sense of purpose, with an emphasis on the reality of Jesus being the Light of the World, the Bread of Life, and the Good Shepherd. There was a moral leadership of persuasion there rather than a leadership of office. What was dearest to him was his conviction of the primacy of Jesus of Nazareth in the life of the world. It drove his spirituality and his life as a priest, especially in presiding at the Eucharist: the re-presentation of the death, resurrection, and ascension of Jesus. But, like St. Francis, he was merely doing what he felt called to.

7

UNDER SIEGE

⁓◦∞◦⁓

F ATHER MYCHAL JUDGE's first assignment was a year's internship at St. Anthony's Shrine, Boston. Although there were still training programs to attend, he said Masses, assisted with the distribution of communion, and heard confessions for two hours at a time. This is what he had always longed to do. "Mychal was always a very sacramental priest," said Jim O'Donnell, who served with him in Boston. "He was very convinced of the power of the sacraments and God's power working through him. He was always going to the sick and blessing them."

Between 1962 and 1966 Father Mychal was assigned to St. Joseph's, East Rutherford, New Jersey, where he worked with young people arranging holy hours, basketball, dances, and bus trips to the World's Fair in New York every Saturday. "In those days the church was the center of their activities," he once said. "Two or three hundred kids at a dance was usual. I could handle crowds of kids."

The Second Vatican Council was gathering at Rome, and Father Mychal kept abreast of its statements. The church was to be viewed essentially as a mystery or sacrament, and not primarily as an institution, something in accord with his own thinking. The church was the whole people of God. God offered salvation to all through other Christian churches and other-than-Christian religions. The Catholic Church was not the only means to salvation, and its official teachings not equally binding. The dignity of the human person was central. The Bible and the liturgy were to underpin the spiritual lives of all members of the church as the main sources of spiritual nourishment. Christians in any state or walk of life were called to "the fullness of Christian life and to the perfection of love." A missionary vision replaced a fortress mentality. Vatican II also gave an impetus to the quest for justice. There was a decree on the renewal of religious life, bringing it more into line with the rest of the church. Members of religious institutes were to "assiduously cultivate" the spirit of prayer and prayer itself, drawing on the authentic sources of Christian spirituality. They were expected to read sacred scripture daily and to meditate on the Word of God. They were to perform the sacred liturgy, especially the mystery of the Holy Eucharist, "with their hearts and lips, according to the mind of the Church, and they should nourish their spiritual lives from this richest of sources."

Between 1967 and 1969, Father Mychal served at Sacred Heart, Rochelle Park, New Jersey, with two other priests. To Michael Randazzo he seemed "like a cool guy" with a sense of fun. He ran the altar boys group and once organized a bus trip to Bertram's Island at Lake Hopatcong. "There was an amusement park there, and he felt we all deserved a fun trip for our service. With a giant roll of tickets, he handed us all a bunch, and off we went into this park to knock ourselves silly on the rides," said Randazzo, now a magician and entertainer.

In the shadow of the death of Martin Luther King Jr., these were still racially turbulent times in the United States. Rochelle Park was an all-white, middle-class town of seven thousand. When its first black family moved in, there were objections from residents, including some members of Sacred Heart. A supportive group in the neighborhood sent around a petition asking people in favor of the black family's presence to sign the form. Mychal Judge happily obliged. " 'Tolerance' at that time was a term that referred to how tight to make a bolt, not how to accept others different from ourselves," Michael Randazzo explained. "But I was a very idealistic kid. There were kids in my school who exhibited very racist ideas, and you knew it came from their parents. I personally never understood why anyone would have a problem with someone of a different race. It just wasn't in me. This good priest signed the petition.

He was different from any priest I had ever met, then or since. He not only told us how to be but proved it in his life and actions."

Because of Father Mychal's open endorsement of the family, however, tensions grew and complaints against him were made to the archdiocese. Suddenly he was removed. A parishioner told me that he had always believed the criticisms came directly from certain members of the church who had objected to Father Mychal's nonracist example: "The complaints were made by racist snobs in the church. He was too dangerous to have around. It was enough to ship him out. Mychal Judge loved too much for these people. He never had a racist bone in his body. It was especially difficult for the children who had gotten to know him and then he was gone. They had to build a whole new relationship with someone else. At that age kids are so impressionable — it didn't seem right to just change things like that."

Father Mychal joined the community back at St. Francis Church in Manhattan as director of the Third Order, or secular Franciscans. The following year, he returned to New Jersey and his former parish of St. Joseph's in East Rutherford, which served twenty-five hundred middle-class families. He seemed to get to know everyone. Inspired by the thinking of Vatican II, he decided to form a team ministry with Jim O'Donnell, Joseph Byrne, and an Italian priest known as Father Justino. It was the first in the Diocese of Newark. "It had nothing to do with rebellion against established authority," he commented. "It's a sharing of responsibilities. Instead of emphasizing our place in the hierarchy, we're emphasizing the quality of our life together, how well we can relate." Each had his areas of responsibility, with any major policy decision discussed and agreed on by the group in weekly meetings. This replaced the traditional notion of obedience, where the pastor made all the decisions and the friars had to ask permission for virtually anything.

Jim O'Donnell recalled: "We worked out things together and divided up the work in the parish. Mike was a team player. I never felt he was doing things on his own. It was a joyful time to live with a leader they called 'Mikey.' He was a very good person who loved the Lord and served him. But it wasn't easy for him all the time. He had been in psychotherapy and he talked to me about it." Father Mychal was drinking during these days, but as Jim O'Donnell pointed out: "At that time everybody drank a lot — even in the order, where it was a form of recreation."

But there was no question of his ever leaving the order, as was the case of O'Donnell and Byrne, who at that time were going through their own transitions. "Mychal was supportive," O'Donnell recalled. "He went out of his way with me when I was going through a struggle about leaving. But he said to me one day that he felt so sad when he walked into my room and saw my habit hanging on the door."

Fathers Justin Eccher, Donan McGovern, Michael Duffy, and Michael Tyson joined the team in the ensuing years. Father Mychal admitted they had problems from time to time, but team ministry helped them cope with the loneliness of not having a family. "This is the greatest bunch of men you'd ever want to have under one roof," he said. "We each have different personalities and our ages range from thirty to seventy, but we're really supportive to one another." Whoever knew the priests personally appreciated the fact that they put in long hours day after day. There were continual calls for help. For each half-hour wedding, there were hours of premarriage counseling and archdiocesan paperwork. "Sometimes I don't take a day off in weeks. There's so much administrative work I don't like."

Father Mychal, who had studied counseling techniques at the American Foundation of Religion and Psychiatry in New York City, was soon to put his negotiating skills to the ultimate test. In May 1974, he and Judge Fred C. Galda found themselves having to confront an armed man who was holding his wife and two children as hostages at their barricaded home in Carlstadt. The siege lasted twelve hours. The two Judges had to try to talk the man into surrendering.

When Father Michael Duffy got back to the friary that day, he was startled to hear the secretary exclaiming: "There's a hostage situation in Carlstadt, and Mychal Judge is up there." He knew only too well that his colleague liked to be where the action was. If Father Mychal heard a fire siren, police car, or dramatic news on the radio, he applied a journalistic instinct to pastoral care.

But this situation broke new ground and was clearly dangerous. Duffy rushed to the scene. When he reached the house he learned that a man on the second floor was pointing a gun to his wife's head as she held a baby in her arms. He was threatening to kill her. Duffy saw a fire truck, lights, police officers, and several other tense-looking people. Then, to his horror, he spotted Mychal Judge in his habit on the top rung of the ladder, talking to the man through the window. "I nearly died because in one hand he had his habit held out because he didn't want to trip, so he was hanging on the ladder with one hand. He wasn't very dexterous anyway."

Duffy watched Judge's head bobbing and heard him saying to the husband: "Well, you know, John, maybe we can work this out. You know this really isn't the way to do it. Why don't you come downstairs and we'll have a cup of coffee and talk this thing over?" Duffy recollected: "We were all there saying, 'He's going to fall off the ladder. There's going to be gunplay.' Not one ounce of fear did he show. But he was telling him: 'You know, you're a good man, John. You don't need to do this.' I don't know what happened but he put the gun down and the wife and the baby's lives were saved. But of course there were cameras there. Wherever there was a photographer within a mile, you could be sure the lens was pointed at Mychal Judge. We used to accuse him of paying the *Bergen Record's* reporter to follow him around."

However, a few months later, when the *Sunday Record* chose Mychal Judge as the subject of a full-page photographic feature for their Lifestyle 74 section, he was careful not to discuss the siege. He told the paper's religion editor that the incident was too personal to talk about in print. He said he had prayed at the time but had not been afraid. "You do what you have to do in such a circumstance, and you don't rationalize."

Many years later the man who had held his family hostage tracked down Father Mychal and invited him to a barbecue. The priest had been the only person who had succeeded in communicating with him. He told friends he was excited about going to the reunion. He considered it a distinct accomplishment that the man had managed to get his life together and was able now to live in a place where he could fry sausages *alfresco.*

The newspaper article gave a revealing glimpse into the life of the handsome forty-one-year-old friar with his "fashionably long hair" and gray streaks that were "beginning to peek through." He was photographed in a variety of locations — relaxing on the lawn with a parishioner, chatting like St. Francis to youngsters and a passing German shepherd, helping a girl on a bicycle cross the road, and sitting with both feet in a grave as he listened to a cemetery worker. Headlined "The Listening Priest" and "A Priest Who Can't Say No," the report focused on Judge's reaction to the turmoil in the church after the changes of Vatican II. He was described as one of the majority of priests who had resisted the mass clergy exodus of the 1960s. He believed that he had more time to serve because he was free from family ties:

> Young kids come to me very idealistically and tell me they want to serve people, and they do. They come and are married, and they still want to serve. And they bring their babies to be baptized, and their ideals have not changed. But the more family responsibilities they gain, the less time they have for others. And that's where celibacy helps. I love being a priest. Sure, I've had my pain, my hurt. I sympathize with priests who have an identity crisis, but I know people need me, and I need them. We're created with body and soul. People need priests to identify with the spiritual.

His fellow priests told the newspaper that Father Mychal worked fourteen hours a day because he could not turn down any request for his time. Mychal Judge said the hardest lesson he had had to learn in his thirteen years as a priest had been letting people be themselves. "Before Vatican II, we were always trying to manage people's lives. 'Do this. Don't do that. Go to Mass. Don't eat meat on Friday.' I was brought up in the old school, and I have to remind myself, 'Mike, let people be.'"

Popes issued encyclicals, bishops formulated policy, but it was the responsibility of the parish priest to communicate the gospel to the people:

> Vatican II put us on the line. In the old days people isolated us on a pedestal. Today, there's a continual challenge for us to do many things, to really be ministers, to bring the sacraments, the Christ life to our people, to counsel — not to give answers but to counsel. You know there are so many people who have no one to talk to, at least no one to confide in. Sometimes we're merely a sounding board. So many people are looking for the spiritual dimension in counseling. I wish I could help more people outside the parish but I don't have time. We don't have any sure answers. We grope. We grow. It strikes me that people are more conscious than ever today that the world needs love; relationships are important.

At the time of the interview, the church was allowing more annulments, having accepted there could be psychological impediments to marriage. Father Mychal disclosed that he was receiving an increasing number of calls from divorced people asking if the church had changed its rules to allow them to remarry in church. He explained that he never gave them a yes-or-no answer over the telephone. He asked them to come to the friary, where they could talk more intimately. He preferred to keep doors open:

> My sin is not having enough hours in the day to follow through with people. I talk to so many. The young kids getting married, the middle-aged with family and marriage problems, the elderly. Sometimes we have three funerals a week, and that means consoling people who we've known a long time. We're a part of their lives, and we can't be

detached at moments of death. At the wakes, the family knows us better than they know the relatives. You're important, and you know it, but it wears you down.

Mychal Judge's interview also gave insights into the tensions within families at the time and how young people were becoming more independently minded.

We get a lot of parents asking what to do about kids fifteen and over who don't want to go to Mass. In the old days, we'd insist. But should we let good family relationships disintegrate because a teenager doesn't want to attend Mass? I try to explain that kids aren't turning off God. We have to look at our culture. The kids are saying no to authority, no to the army, and now, without the draft summons, many are saying no to college; they're saying no to IBM careers. There's only one thing that turns them on, and that's travel. Look how many kids are going to Europe. We made a world of wheels, and they're traveling on them.

Father Mychal felt young people were doing religion their own way. He believed them when they said they talked to God and prayed. He knew they needed the church. God's grace was always available. "He'll guide them. He established a church, gave us the sacraments. We have to leave the kids in God's hands. He has his own way of working. A good liturgy, guitar Masses, sure they are a means of bringing youth to church, but they aren't the answer for all."

In a short section on preaching, Father Mychal reflected on the art of the sermon. "We have to be versatile in preaching. If I'm giving a homily and a fire truck goes by with ringing siren, I switch my original thoughts and relate to what's happening — the fire — and what could be a distraction becomes an asset."

That same month, September 1974, Mychal Judge received tragic news about a close friend since his teenage years. Father Noel Fitzpatrick, who had achieved leadership roles within the

Franciscan community, died of a heart attack, aged thirty-nine. He had been ordained for only thirteen years. According to Father Edward Flanagan, his death had a noticeable impact on Mychal Judge:

> I remember his very human grieving at the loss of a friend whom he had known for twenty-five years but also a sense of faith that Noel had gone off to be with God. It was also the loss of deep brotherhood. The death was something that touched him a lot and had an influence on his own attitude toward death: that life is fragile and none of us knows when God is going to call us. Mychal believed in taking advantage of one day at a time and doing your best to be there for what you think God wants you to do — to live out faith that way. Noel's death was very hard to understand because he was just beginning to achieve all the potential that was there. He not only had great promise but had already achieved much. He would have gone on to have a lot of responsibility in the Franciscan community.

From an ecclesiological perspective, Mychal Judge felt that the 1970s were the most exciting era in the history of the church. "The whole world has changed; the church is growing, and I'm maturing," he said. "People want to talk about religion at barbecues. Years ago the church was a one-way street, but now there are so many different personalities, mentalities. The human mind is a fascinating thing. How boring the world would be if we were all alike." He also explained the need to get away. He would go into the countryside on "healing missions," regaining a sense of perspective through the experience of a simple hill or mountain climb and then being able to go back down into the valley with a renewed spirit.

During his time in East Rutherford, however, secret heavy drinking sessions helped to anaesthetize inner pain. A friend explained that whenever Mychal Judge and a former classmate had an evening and a day off together, they would visit multiple Irish bars on Third Avenue and stay overnight at a friary.

When he was in his best form, Mychal Judge communicated a simplicity of living that impressed even his fellow friars. His clothes were always pressed and clean, but he never owned much. As St. Francis had said, to have possessions was, in a sense, to be possessed by them. This detachment from materialism might have provided the impetus for his attachment to people. An illustration of this was his desire to bless women and men physically, even if they didn't request it. An elderly lady would come up to him, and he'd talk to her as though she were the only person on the earth. Then he would say, "Let me give you a blessing." He would place his big thick Irish hands on her head and press down. Then he would look up to heaven and ask God to bless her and give her health and peace. If a young couple approached him and announced they were to become parents, he would put his hand on the woman's stomach and call on God to bless the unborn child. If a fellow priest were taking teenagers on a bus trip, he would stay around until the coach was about to leave, then jump on board, lead the teenagers in prayer, and bless them for a safe and happy journey. Or when a husband and wife were in crisis, he might take both their hands at the same time, put them next to his and whisper a blessing in the hope that the crisis might soon be over.

Fifteen hundred parishioners attended his farewell party in East Rutherford in 1976. Valedictory notes ranged from "I'll miss you so much because you were always there" to "You won't be here to bury me." Michael Duffy commented: "He loved to bring Christ to people. He was the bridge between people and God."

8

ADDICTION AND GRACE

⁓⁓

THOSE WHO KNEW Mychal Judge as the ever willing pastor, relentlessly helping others, would not have been aware of the extent to which he needed to help himself. His alcoholism had become so serious that, according to Stephen Weaver, it presented him with both a crisis and an opportunity:

> He was living existentially on a knife-edge, functioning as a priest yet painfully aware of his need to drink. Sometimes knowing that he was unable to function properly, he would still go out and conduct a funeral or baptism. He recalled some of the archetypal figures in American mythology, such as Judy Garland, who would sing her torch song despite being much the worse for wear — and carry far more passion because of it.

The drinking had intensified as he had moved from the confines of his formation period into a greater measure of independence in his pastoral appointments. Matters were to come to a head when he was appointed assistant to the president of Siena College in Loudonville, New York, in the fall of 1976. With twenty-five hundred full-time undergraduate students, the college educated young men and women in arts, sciences, and business. The authorities had wanted to make an external appointment to bring a new perspective to campus life. With his ability to relate to people and his experience of parish ministry, Mychal Judge seemed the right person.

The priest who had always felt insecure about his lack of intellectual prowess had become part of the academic establishment, even if his role were primarily a fund-raising one. He found it hard to believe that he was working at one of the Franciscan flagships of learning in the Holy Name Province.

Mychal Judge reported to the president, Father Hugh Hines, and represented him to any number of constituencies. He was well liked and respected by the students, staff, and trustees. As an intermediary, he dealt with complaints effectively. He was also skilled at representing the school in the CICU — the Commission on Independent Colleges and Universities for the State of New York. "Once Siena was called to represent the 120 independent schools, so Mychal acted as a lobbyist," Father Hines recalled. "Sometimes the state senators and the assembly members would know him and not me. He was very good at public relations." But Mychal Judge did not relish the administration side so much. College budgets cannot have been appealing to a man who gave his money away, and state education reports were not the forms of giving and receiving to which he was naturally inclined. He would say that unless he actually saw the students in the dormitory, it was easy to forget what college life was all about.

He chose to live in a student dormitory. His pastoral work there was among out-of-town students who stayed at the college during the week. Being a housefather in a "freshman women's dorm" was a "tremendous experience" as was the informal contact with students, he once said. He loved to celebrate the sacraments, including baptisms and weddings, at Siena. "I married a number of those girls," he would tell friends proudly.

Father Hines explained how the staff had not realized the priest's extraordinary capacity for work:

> Time was nothing to him. If he had to be somewhere at 7:00 A.M. he would be there, even if a student had turned up at his room at 11:30 the night before. On Sunday evenings he would have a small Mass in his room, where the students would gather round a table. He had a gift for counseling students in a nondirective way. He was always looking at different options for students who were struggling.

But he was struggling too. During his time at Siena he decided to join Alcoholics Anonymous. He talked to Hugh Hines about his problem:

> I knew he drank — many people do socially — but I was not aware of his alcoholism because he never missed a beat of his job. I think for people of his age it was part of the Irish culture. He was so overworked when he was in the parish. He would come home at night and have a drink or two. One night a student from Siena was killed in an accident, and security had called him. He was so happy that he had not had a drink because he was able to make the hour's journey and inform the parents. Three or four days later he told me he had joined A.A.
>
> It was under control. I think talking to students helped him. They shared their struggles with each other. He saw some people going down the primrose path. Some may have said he was drinking too much, but when I was with him I was not aware of it. He was always very professional.

ALCOHOLICS ANONYMOUS was born in June 1935. Its founders, Bill Wilson and Dr. Bob Smith, wrote *The Twelve Steps*, drawing on the wealth of their own insights as well as the collective wisdom of philosophers and cultures. These principles offered simple, straightforward guidance to men and women wanting to lead sober lives. The steps were intended only as suggestions for living, not as requirements for membership. They were guides to recovery, supporting people in accepting their powerlessness over alcohol. Honesty about the past and the present was fundamental to the recovery process. The Steps encouraged members to embrace the concept of a Power greater than themselves in handling everyday stress and, if lived well, promised "miraculous changes."

Mychal Judge attended his first meeting of A.A. in Albany on June 15, 1978. The chair would have asked if there were any newcomers, visitors, or "people who are coming back." The priest

The Twelve Steps of Alcoholics Anonymous

1. We admitted we were powerless over alcohol — that our lives had become unmanageable.

2. Came to believe that a Power greater than ourselves could restore us to sanity.

3. Made a decision to turn our will and our lives over to the care of God *as we understood Him*.

4. Made a searching and fearless moral inventory of ourselves.

5. Admitted to God, to ourselves, and to another human being the exact nature of our wrongs.

6. Were entirely ready to have God remove all these defects of character.

7. Humbly asked Him to remove our shortcomings.

8. Made a list of all the persons we had harmed, and became willing to make amends to them all.

9. Made direct amends to such people wherever possible, except when to do so would injure them or others.

10. Continued to take personal inventory and when we were wrong promptly admitted it.

11. Sought through prayer and meditation to improve our conscious contact with God *as we understood Him*, praying only for knowledge of His will for us and the power to carry that out.

12. Having had a spiritual awakening as the result of these steps, we tried to carry this message to alcoholics, and to practice these principles in all our affairs.

---

might have introduced himself with "My name is Mychal, and I'm an alcoholic." He would have stayed after the meeting to exchange phone numbers, join a group, and get a sponsor. The A.A. preamble would have been read:

Alcoholics Anonymous is a fellowship of men and women who share their experience, strength, and hope with each other that they may solve their common problem and help others to recover from alcoholism.

The only requirement for membership is a desire to stop drinking. There are no dues or fees in A.A. We are self-supporting through our own contributions. A.A. is not allied with any sect, denomination, politics, organization, or institution; does not wish to engage in any controversy; neither endorses nor opposes any causes. Our primary purpose is to stay sober and help other alcoholics to achieve sobriety.

Every new member was expected to attend ninety meetings in ninety days, so the organization could be seen almost as a cate-chumenate for converts to sobriety — a safe place to learn about the disease of alcoholism and fellowship of A.A. Mychal Judge learned how A.A. distinguished between social, heavy, and alcoholic drinking and how only an individual member could tell the difference. He understood that alcoholism was a physical, mental, and spiritual disease: "We're as sick as our secrets," he would say. He knew that the process of recovery meant more than being "dry" and that sobriety could bring peace of mind, freedom, and joy in the service of others.

At the heart of its nondenominational and nondogmatic spirituality was the need for honesty, willingness, and self-acceptance. At A.A. Mychal Judge engaged with himself in authentic acts of self-love. They were times of self-care when he could be truthful in recognizing his limitations. He was able to say: "I am an addict. I am out of control. This is beyond me." He found the fellowship constructive and supportive. He would say to his Franciscan brothers: "I need to go to a meeting." It became a catchphrase. The need was internal because he was in touch with a deeper dimension of being. Whatever each day brought in terms of frustration or stress, he was faithful to A.A., attending up to five meetings a week and often speaking at them. A fellow Franciscan told me that, after learning about A.A. from Father Mychal, his own ministry benefited: "Mychal used to say, 'I was once a drunk myself. So stop drinking, go to a meeting, work the steps, get a sponsor, and work one day at a time.' That became a divine source of spiritual renewal, regeneration, and revivification."

At each hour-long meeting, Mychal would experience different dimensions of A.A. He heard thousands of testimonies over the years through beginners' meetings, men's meetings, women's meetings, step meetings, topic meetings (when the leader would choose a theme such as fear or gratitude), and eleventh-step meditation meetings with silent group prayer and sharing.

Attending gatherings in different parts of the United States and absorbing its literature soon formed part of his regular meditative practice. A.A. nurtured him in a way neither Catholicism nor Franciscanism did. He found himself inspired by other people's journeys and the spiritual disciplines of those in recovery. In the language of A.A, these were challenges of openness, letting go, forgiving, accepting, becoming selfless, and reaching out to others. Whether eating muffins with Bill Clinton at the White House, meeting Gerry Adams in Belfast, or taking pilgrims to the healing shrine of Lourdes in southwest France, Mychal Judge would check out where the nearest A.A. meeting was likely to be. It was a community to which he felt he owed his life.

After meetings, he would go to diners with members to celebrate birthdays and anniversaries. Many of the friends in his life were people he had met in the meetings of A.A. across the world. While Mychal was undoubtedly a giver, he was also someone who was nurtured, fed, received, cared for, loved, and supported by his brothers and sisters on the journey of recovery. Even those friends who were not alcoholics would notice the spiritual impact A.A. was having on his life: "When we would travel together and share a room," recalled Hugh Hines, "I would jump into bed. But he would be up reading the Bible and one of the A.A. books. He would then get on his knees and tell me I should get out of bed and do some praying too. He would say, 'It's just a nice way to end the day with these prayers.' "

The recognition of the role of grace became an essential component in Mychal Judge's move from addiction to sobriety. In his

book *Addiction and Grace,* Dr. Gerald May analyzes these con-
cepts from a spiritual viewpoint. Addiction exists, he maintains,
wherever people are internally compelled to give energy to issues
that are not their true desires. It is a state of compulsion, obses-
sion, or preoccupation that enslaves a person's will and ultimately
eclipses the energy of a desire for love and goodness. In the sense,
however, that addiction brings people to their knees, it can be
owned as a gift. Failure is a necessary step because only through
such resignation can people most honestly and completely turn
to grace. Grace — "the invincible advocate of freedom and the
absolute expression of perfect love" — is the only hope, May
argued, for dealing with addiction. It was the only power that can
overcome its destructive force. Grace is a dynamic outpouring of
God's loving nature flowing into and through creation in a continual self-offering of healing, love, illumination, and reconciliation.
Addictions fill up the spaces where grace might flow.

As well as providing a means for Father Mychal to confront and
address his alcoholism, the grace of A.A. meetings enabled him to
look deep within himself, perhaps for the first time, and face the personal history that haunted him. The first issue was the relationship
with his mother. Father Mychal told Stephen Weaver that, while his
mother had supported her son's decision to become a Franciscan,
she had continued to play a somewhat domineering role in his life:

> Mychal very dutifully responded to those demands and
> would accompany her on holidays but would talk about these
> vacations as very painful experiences in which she would
> rehearse her dependent nature and he would respond as a
> codependent. As Mychal also struggled with alcoholism, he
> was locked into that codependent relationship for most of
> his adult life. The death of his mother enabled him to real-
> ize his real giftedness — that he could achieve from his own
> strengths and weaknesses in a way that would have made
> her proud. By then, he was free of the need to physically
> demonstrate anything to his mother.

Mychal Judge agreed that Irish guilt was a contributory cause of his alcoholism. It concerned issues of self-esteem, self-worth, and striving for perfection. "It is in my judgment — and only in my judgment — a cultural and genetic factor," said Frank Murphy:

> The people most prone to alcoholism — American Indians, Irish, Russians, Poles — are races that have had their self-esteem taken away over the centuries. Mychal and I talked about this in relation to our parents. We were both recovering alcoholics and suffered from self-esteem issues. We could almost open our souls to each other. We also found that we shared great humor. I think we were helpful to each other. Periodically he suffered internally. He may have had depression but he was such an outgoing personality and we had so much humor in common. We could make each other laugh all the time.

Brendan Fay felt it would be difficult to ascertain precisely what Mychal Judge had been trying to escape from through drinking. For each alcoholic there were different stories and motivations. Every member turned up at the A.A. meetings intent on sobriety and, having found it, began a journey of recovery. "It's not so much about finding the root causes of alcoholism but about acceptance," he said:

> Within the recovery movement he found a community of people, a safe space where he could be himself for the first time in his life. Slowly and surely, all the things he had hidden or denied about himself were in the open and the real Mychal Judge could find a home for himself. Wherever he was in the world, he would seek out the places where he would meet other brothers and sisters on their journeys of recovery. He knew A.A. brought him back to the place where he could truly be his most honest self.

In touch with his own sexual identity, the priest had the mettle to attend meetings of A.A. that comprised mainly gay people. "This took some guts," said a Franciscan friend. "It had to do with his sense of authentic selfhood, of taking care of one's self."

Fay added that Mychal Judge had to make distinctions between where to be honest, when to be honest, and how to be honest. There was a world of difference between rigorous honesty and reckless honesty. While never naïve about his own background and experience, he learned how to be wise, sensible, and prudent. He thought deeply, and yet no doubt once he had found himself at home among that community celebrating the gift of sobriety and recovery he was as committed to that journey of honesty. Not only did he find himself helped by many people, a new ministry of helping other alcoholics opened up. Many of the friends he forged bonds with in the last decades of his life were also recovering alcoholics.

While Mychal Judge was one of many priest members of A.A., it was difficult for people outside the organization to understand exactly the effect it was having on his spiritual life as a religious. Perhaps a sense can be gleaned from a Catholic nun who has been a member for many years. In her book *Seeds of Grace*, Sister Molly Monahan (a pseudonym), describes how A.A. brought her new life precisely as a Catholic. She writes:

> My Catholicism is as much a part of my identity as is my alcoholism. It is the mother tongue of my soul, and the "language" of its creed, code, and cult (worship) articulate and give me ways to express the spirituality I find in A.A. . . . From the beginning I "saw" A.A. spirituality through the lens of my Catholic faith, as it were, and tested it for its soundness against my understanding and apprecia-tion of the Catholic tradition. . . . As a Catholic, because of my belief in the incarnation of Jesus Christ, his taking on and sanctifying human flesh and all matter, I know that my body, ever so really part of me, is holy too. And it needs to have a part in my worship of God in word, song, gesture. My senses — of seeing, hearing, tasting, touching, smelling —

need the spiritual nourishment provided by the music, the sacred vestments and vessels, the bread, wine, water, oils, candles, incense, flowers. They need the painting, frescoes, mosaics, the sculpture inspired by scripture and tradition.

It is probable that Mychal Judge felt the same way because he was at heart a sacramental priest rooted in liturgical tradition. His regular attendance at meetings was probably a means of his being able to be himself in an environment where he felt accepted and secure.

Senator Tom Duane had often detected insecurities lurking beneath the self-confident exterior.

There was an expression that I am sure he used in A.A: "Don't compare your insides to other people's outsides." He had a wonderful outside, but that only leads me to believe he had a complicated and perhaps difficult inside. He did have the sickness of addiction. Addiction does make people's experience in life more unusual than the average citizen's. It leaves you with a certain loneliness, a certain isolation, and a certain need to reach out to fill that isolation and loneliness that might be felt.

Mychal Judge's acceptance of his addiction propelled him into a mission to help others. Stepping over the trap of self-abasement, he proceeded along a path of honesty and humility. The journey was not so much the story of a soul but the recovery of a self.

9

DIGNITY AND COMPASSION

—∞∞∞—

THE PILGRIMAGE was soon to open up a contradiction between himself and the church that had nurtured him. Those demons of self-doubt hovered at every crossroads, but the courage with which he fought them off was to have profound consequences. The spiritual dimension of A.A. helped Mychal own his sexuality.

He had followed coverage of the Stonewall Riots in June 1969, which had led to the birth of the gay liberation movement in the United States. In the ensuing years, he supported the activities of Dignity, a community of lesbian, gay, bisexual, and transgendered Catholics and their friends who gathered weekly for Mass. They held social events and devised an active program of social outreach. A branch of Dignity USA, the Dignity/New York chapter was formed in 1972 by the priest John McNeill. With the purpose of encouraging gay men, lesbians, bisexual, and transgendered people "to express their sexuality in a manner that is consonant with Christ's teaching," Dignity helped them become more active members of the Roman Catholic Church and of society as a whole. As a movement, it worked through education and legal reform for justice and social acceptance. At the same time, members accepted their responsibilities to the church, to their Catholic heritage, to society, and to each other.

Dignity was instrumental in setting up the National Gay Task Force, which in 1973 convinced St. Vincent's Catholic Hospital in New York to enact the first hospital sexual orientation nondiscrimination policy in employment and patient care. In 1974 the chapter began annual attempts to help pass a gay civil rights law by rallying groups of supportive clergy and sending priests and nuns to testify in favor of the bill, a move that encountered strong opposition from the Archdiocese of New York.

Between 1979 and 1987, Dignity met at St. Francis Xavier Roman Catholic Church. Father Mychal Judge attended the gatherings and made many new friends. He was attached to the priests' support group, which was also involved in social justice and civil rights issues through both its community and its HIV/AIDS outreach programs. In his early years of sobriety, he particularly supported recovering alcoholics who were gay. "The first five years of sobriety were very hard," said Ted Patterson. "We cared for one another. We made one another laugh. I was not too faithful to the church at that time. In fact, I was mad at it. I was losing my faith. He made me believe again. I think he gave me God. He always waited for those who came out of the church hurt." Bill Burt remembered his saying: "We have got everything going for us. We are gay. We are alcoholics. We can really do it if we want to. It's a good thing, not a bad thing."

Although unstintingly compassionate to individuals, Mychal Judge was always politically astute in terms of his own public persona. He resumed parish life in 1979 — this time in a rural setting, serving as guardian and pastor of St. Joseph's, West Milford, New Jersey. It was situated forty-five miles from New York City at Echo Lake, from where the stone for the Brooklyn Bridge buttresses had been quarried. A heavily wooded neighborhood in reservoir land, the parish dated to 1765 and was the oldest Catholic community in New Jersey.

While there was poverty as well as ongoing pastoral problems to address, parishioners indicated that it was perhaps not the most natural place for Mychal Judge. There are indications that he might have felt isolated there, not least because another world was opening up to him in New York City. Parishioner Tom Ferriter, who regarded him as a quintessential New Yorker with a slight Brooklyn pugnaciousness, confessed: "He hated being a pastor here. He was used to the big life in New York."

Father Mychal's sense of displacement seems to have emerged after only two weeks when he approached Tom Ferriter after Mass and asked what he was doing that day. Ferriter told him he was going to see his mother, who lived on Long Island, a three-hour journey away. Ferriter recounted:

> She was getting old and a little difficult. I told him she was from County Leitrim in Ireland. "My mother's from Leitrim," he said, asking me what time I was going. I said, "Three o'clock — three hours there and three hours back." Mychal said, "Gee, You've got a long day."
> My wife and I came out at three o clock and we got into the big Buick. I started the car up and felt a movement at the back. Being from New York City, I thought we were being hijacked. I turned around and it was Mychal Judge. He just got in the back of the car and said, "Let's go." We drove out to Long Island and had a delightful conversation. When we got to my mother's house, he told my wife and I to go out for a meal while he talked to my mother. We went inside, but he shooed us out of the house. "Call me before you come back." About an hour later I called, and he said: "Not yet." We went off for another hour and I called again: "Not yet." Three hours into the visit, I called once more, and he said, "Okay, you can come over." When we got back, my mother was purring like a kitten. He was sitting at the table with the tea. It was all very Irish, and they had the rosaries out. Up to that point she had been difficult, but now she was beautiful. And she was beautiful for another year. It was unbelievable. I don't know what he did. I think she wanted people to pay attention to her and be stroked over her old Irish Catholicism. I think he understood and from then on I owed him my soul.

During his first year, the Ferriters held a Christmas party and invited Father Mychal to their home. Everyone was in festive spirit, but there was no sign of the priest. The party was about to draw to a close when Father Mychal's car pulled up at midnight. "Where were you?" asked Ferriter. "Give me a cup of coffee, please," Judge replied.

I'm so embarrassed. I didn't know where you lived exactly. I know I had been here when we drove out to Long Island, but I forgot where you lived. I saw the first house with all the cars in front of it, so I walked in with my brown habit and sandals. Somebody gave me a glass of ginger ale. I was looking for you and Noreen, and everybody else I know, but I couldn't see anyone I recognized. Then I heard someone say: "I didn't know this was a costume party." Then I realized I was at the wrong address.

It wasn't the first time Father Mychal's attire had been mistaken for fancy dress. Some years earlier, at another party, he was assumed to be a male stripper who had turned up disguised as a friar. He wore his habit as a sign of witness: "You can wear that robe any place in the world," he would say. "People stop and talk to you and open up the depths of their hearts. It is not me as a person, but the tradition of the friars. You always find a colorful person inside that brown robe."

Charlie Galanaugh remembered that Mychal Judge would always try to find a way of evading social events. He enjoyed having a good time but always felt "a little guilty" if he wasn't helping someone in need. "We have a family of five children who loved him and called him Uncle Mikey. He loved to see a beautiful family that apparently didn't have any major disabling problems. He liked to spend time with us at the house. But he almost would have preferred it had we had some major problem to try to solve."

Most people in the West Milford parish were attracted by Father Mychal's charm. He was a friar for everybody and had a prayer for all seasons. He always had simple points to make in his homilies, yet the congregation discerned great wisdom and humanity. They were affected by his presence. He spoke from the aisle without notes. He was nervous beforehand, a trait his performance belied.

In church he had a calming influence. He would speak loudly on occasions and could make points dramatically, perhaps turning toward a particular individual. There was something of the actor in him, but his style was not primarily theatrical. When he spoke, the phrases were accessible and connected with the people. He would say things like "I love you" as if he were addressing an individual personally. "He used to walk around a lot when he talked," Dolly Galanaugh observed. "He would go down the aisles, always putting his hand inside the white rope, which went around his habit, and clutching on to that. He moved his arms around a lot. He said sometimes he thought he should have been Italian."

Mychal Judge saw the role of a Franciscan "to be today, to be this moment, to keep the gospel message, bring hope and life, to preach and renew." He said he found preaching easier the older he became. "I've absorbed a lot of life and information. I'm putting it together and offering it back to people."

He was a man who prayed and moved, often at the same time. Father Edward Flanagan, then serving in a parish ten miles away, remembered stopping by at the friary one day, only to find Mychal Judge out in the parking lot walking up and down. "He was praying the liturgy of the hours or the rosary. He was walking quickly. Mike never did anything slowly. He was always a man on the run."

But he did not rush confessions. More children lined up outside his box than any other because they loved to talk with him. He would go out of his way to treat them equally. When Sister Jean Hekker took over the students' preparation for the sacrament of confirmation, the candidates were required to write Father Mychal a letter asking permission to receive the sacrament. Sister Jean recalled that he answered all their letters with a personally hand-written note. To make sure all the candidates received their replies from him on the same day, the evening before he drove from one post office to another (Butler, West Milford, Oak Ridge, and Newfoundland) making sure the envelopes would all have the same mailing date. "I found him to be a good listener and a kind friend," she said. "He was someone with sensitive feelings and a true Franciscan."

Although Father Mychal knew he had responsibilities to parish life, he was always eager to minister in less obvious ways. When he attended the Winter Olympics in Lake Placid, for example, he noticed a look of loneliness on some skaters' faces. People instinctively ignored them because they thought they would not want to be disturbed. But Mychal Judge looked deeper. He could always sense when people were genuinely anxious or in psychological pain. So he decided to go up to the skaters and break the ice. They appeared calmed by his approach and told him they appreciated his gesture. "He went to suffering the way moths go to fire," said Charlie Galanaugh.

In an interview with the *West Milford Argus* in November 1984, Mychal Judge reflected that he was the richest man in the world because of "the people I've met, and joys and pains I've shared with them, and the times in which I've lived." It was a "wonderful time" to be alive in the church: "Bishops are on the front page of the *New York Times* because the world is looking to the church for moral leadership — who else can give it? If you are in the church today, you are automatically a leader."

His leadership in West Milford was tested when a local Catholic school announced to him that it was having difficulty meeting its financial and educational objectives. As pastor, he had to take responsibility. He saw the church's mission as educational but wondered how much energy should be expended on a small subsection of the parish comprising a few hundred children. While certainly not opposed to Catholic education, he was struggling with whether or not this was the right use of resources and wondered whether the school should be closed. Charlie Galanaugh recalled:

> There was a faction who did not like him because he ultimately concluded that we might have to abandon the school. A group of people gave him a great deal of grief over that.

Those committed to Catholic education felt he was not giving them the support they thought they needed, and there
was some conflict. The bishop's representative came and did
a fact-finding study. He sided clearly with the school rather
than Mychal, who was under a lot of pressure.

MYCHAL JUDGE was nearing the end of his six-year stint at
West Milford and becoming increasingly frustrated by the parish
machine. He knew he had pastoral gifts, but the context could
no longer contain them. Moreover, his friendship with fellow gay
Christians was at the same time making him restless and giving him new confidence. In 1984 press and television coverage
zeroed in on the mayor's Executive Order #50, which forbade
discrimination against gays or lesbians from employers who did
business with the city or received city funding. The taxes they paid
were not to be used to discriminate against them in employment.
A Catholic priest friend, Father Bernard Lynch, made headlines
that set him at odds with Archbishop John O'Connor, who had
opposed the order. Lynch saw employment as a basic human right
for all people. The *New York Post* quoted the archbishop as saying, "[I would] close all my orphanages rather than employ one
gay person." Lynch considered this a "particularly vile statement."
By citing orphanages as an example, the archbishop "may have
left the impression that gayness was to be equated with child
molestation — something that was anathema to everyone, gay
and heterosexual alike."

The battle lines between the church and the gay community
were being drawn. Mychal Judge felt torn. Perhaps he needed time
to explore the implications of his sexuality away from the American context. He had also grown tired of parish life and felt a
period of renewal was due. With the permission of his order, he
wrote a carefully worded letter of application to the Franciscan
International Study Centre in Canterbury, England. Enclosing a
copy of the *West Milford Argus* feature — "to get an idea of who I
am" — he asked to be "updated in theology and scripture, to sit

and listen, absorb and share." The spirit of his application revealed a friar eager to fly: "I realize that the courses might be a great challenge — I'll take it! Everything in class and out of class will be used for living, preaching, ministry, and teaching." The application explained how he had been associated with Franciscanism since he was fourteen and how he had been a priest for nearly a quarter of a century: "It is my life. Perhaps too I could bring some pastoral experience and share with others from different ministries."

Mychal Judge seemed determined to cross the Atlantic. He wanted to experience Franciscanism in a new culture and looked forward to attending meetings of Alcoholics Anonymous in England. Moreover, this passage from pages 83–84 of the book *Alcoholics Anonymous* impelled him forward:

> We are going to know a new freedom and a new happiness. We will not regret the past nor wish to shut the door on it. We will comprehend the word serenity and we will know peace. No matter how far down the scale we have gone, We will see how our experience can benefit others. That feeling of uselessness and self-pity will disappear. We will lose interest in selfish things and gain interest in our fellows. Self-seeking will slip away. Our whole attitude and outlook on life will change. Fear of people and of economic insecurity will leave us. We will intuitively know how to handle situations which used to baffle us. We will suddenly realize that God is doing for us what we could not do for ourselves.

When Mychal Judge's application was accepted, he was overjoyed and believed the sabbatical would be an occasion to reflect on the precepts. In many ways his time in England would be a watershed — and he was soon to find out who his friends were.

A shepherd who laid down his life for his flock: Father Mychal Judge being carried away from the World Trade Center site on the morning of September 11, 2001.

On the edge of the deep: Father Mychal Judge chatting with a cemetery worker at Lyndhurst while serving at St. Joseph's, East Rutherford, New Jersey, in 1974.

In the spirit of St. Francis: Father Mychal Judge befriending an Alsatian as he meets youngsters in East Rutherford, New Jersey, 1974.

Popular pastor: Father Mychal Judge sharing a hug with parishioner Mae Reilly of St. Joseph's Church, West Milford, New Jersey, 1982.

The European:
Father Mychal Judge during
a visit to Mont St. Michel,
Normandy, in June 1995.

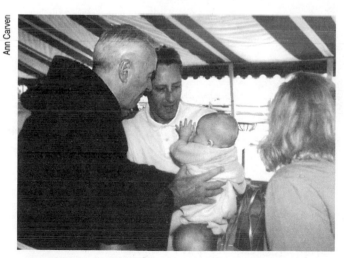

Honoring the victims of TWA Flight 800 at Smith Point, Long Island, 1998.
Father Mychal Judge with Jay Carven, Ethan Carven, and Ann Carven.

Beyond the call of duty: Father Mike, the New York City Fire Chaplain, 1999.

"I promised him prayers
each morning and night."
Father Mychal Judge with
President Bill Clinton at the
annual breakfast for religious
leaders at the White House
in September 1999.

Instruments of Peace: Father Mychal Judge with Steven McDonald and
the Bruderhof's choir, "Kids for Peace," on the "Journey to Forgiveness"
in Northern Ireland, 2000.

An eye for the camera: Father Mychal with his friend Stephen Weaver, during a visit to San Francisco in September 2000.

The grave of Father Mychal Judge at Holy Sepulchre Cemetery, Totowa, New Jersey.

Part Three

CHARISM
OF THE WOUNDS

And then Christ said to me: "Do you know what I have done to you? I have given you the emblems of My Passion so that you may be my standard-bearer."

— *The Fifth Consideration on the Holy Stigmata*

10

CANTERBURY TALES

⎯⎯∞⎯⎯

THE NEW FIFTY-TWO-YEAR-OLD STUDENT looked more like a Hollywood director than a religious brother. The brown habit had been cast off in favor of a denim jacket with an upturned collar and blue jeans. A gold-earring dangled from the left lobe, and the bouffant hairstyle seemed only enhanced by shades of gray. This was to be the mode of Mychal Judge's gap year in Canterbury.

Father Anthony McNeill, then a student training for the priesthood, remembered observing a "charismatic guy with his hair swept back" standing in the courtyard of the Franciscan International Study Centre: "I didn't think he was a friar. I thought this was someone a little bit out of the ordinary — and he was. He was like a magnet, full of life, very free and liberated in his thinking. He could well have been a film producer, not a stereotypical priest in any way."

The cobbled city of Canterbury lies in East Kent in the southeast corner of England. The seat of the Anglican archbishop and primate of England, it was the starting point for St. Augustine's mission to the country in A.D. 597. After St. Thomas à Becket was murdered in the Norman cathedral in 1170, it became a place of pilgrimage inspiring Geoffrey Chaucer to write *The Canterbury Tales*. The city is also home to the University of Kent. The study center lies on the fringe of the campus.

Father Austin McCormack, who was principal at the time, said that Mychal had come as a friar seeking spiritual renewal. Among the courses he attended were those focusing on Franciscan spirituality and human development. He was eager to provide input from his own experience: "He was a giant of a man with an enormous heart. He lived life to the full, and what was perhaps even more important to him than that was his desire to help others do the same. Wherever there was a difficulty, he was in there trying to help. He was a man who saw his limitations as a capacity for gift. Like St. Francis he found so much good to celebrate because he expected to find it — and he went looking for it."

Some speculated on the underlying reasons for his sabbatical. There were those who suspected he had become tired of being a conventional parish priest. Others sensed tensions within his own Franciscan community back in America. Whatever the truth, Mychal Judge's spell in the United Kingdom was to be a time of replenishment and rediscovery. Even zaniness. He signed on for aerobics classes and took to the stage.

The year also coincided with the silver jubilee of his ordination to the priesthood and was therefore a convenient resting place on his pilgrimage. By now Henri Nouwen's *The Wounded Healer* had become a classic of pastoral care and was on every priest's bookshelf. Nouwen had encouraged ministers to make their psychological wounds a source of healing for others. This did not mean sharing superficial pains but a constant willingness to see one's own suffering as rising from the depth of the human condition. A minister was not a doctor, whose primary task was to relieve pain, but someone who could deepen pain to a level where it could be shared in the context of hospitality and community. For Nouwen, loneliness was a wound easily subject to denial and neglect. But once the pain was accepted and understood, it could form the basis for a healing ministry:

> It is healing because it takes away the false illusion that wholeness can be given by one to another. It is healing because it does not take away the loneliness and pain of another, but invites him to recognize his loneliness on a level where it can be shared. Many people in this life suffer because they are anxiously searching for the man or woman, the event or encounter, which will take their loneliness away.

But when they enter a house with real hospitality they soon see that their own wounds must be understood not as sources of despair and bitterness, but as signs that they have to travel on in obedience to the calling sounds of their own wounds.

THE CANTERBURY SOJOURN enabled Mychal Judge to summon the courage to pursue that pastoral vision. But it was not an easy adjustment, and he passed through several tunnels in the process. The interconnection of spirituality and sexuality was one of the great breakthroughs he had made in terms of his human and spiritual development. He had always been a person of deep faith who had pursued his vocation with authenticity and single-mindedness. But it was only when he had begun to recognize that his sexuality had been repressed and in some sense denied that he could integrate it into his ministry and priesthood. He knew this would make him an even more authentic person. Close friends say his sojourn was partly to reflect on the significance of that and to consolidate it.

He later described his time in England as "the extraordinary challenging year." It was an opportunity to enjoy his newfound freedom as a sober recovering alcoholic and as one coming to terms with his sexuality. He was excited to be experiencing a different culture through the galleries and attractions of London and to have the chance to cross the channel and discover non-English-speaking cultures as well.

Friends from those days spoke of his physical appearance, which seemed to symbolize the inner mood: "There was a kind of vanity about the way he looked," said Father George Smulski. "He certainly acted young. He was trying to present or create a persona or image. I think he was changing that year. He was carving out a new Franciscan life for himself. But he was happy about being a friar."

Yet for all his immaculate personal style, his living quarters at Canterbury were always "an absolute pit," according to Brian Purfield, a fellow friar at Canterbury. "The bed was unmade. There were clothes all over the place. That's how he lived. He got out of stuff, into something else, and moved on."

Mychal, known in later years for living in uncluttered rooms, was evidently entering a carefree period. He did not give the impression of being weighed down with anxiety — publicly at any rate: "I never saw him without a smile on his face," secretary and receptionist Fay Mactavish told me. "He was always jolly and his eyes sparkled." Staff and students often heard him laughing in the corridor. He moved around the center at a "gentle pace" and had time for everyone.

Brian Purfield, then a student fresh from the Franciscan novitiate, joined Mychal Judge for a course in theological renewal, the effects of Vatican II, and pastoral ministry. There were twenty-five students comprising friars, sisters of different congregations, and lay people: "He was loud. You knew he was around. He was a great organizer in bringing the group together. People who were shy were a natural target for him. He just brought them in."

While his half-rimmed spectacles made him look academic, it has to be said that study was not high on his list of priorities. He wore the glasses while preaching; he knew they made him look learned, and he played into that. Fellow Franciscans occasionally found him difficult to "read" as a homilist because he could so naturally mock in a total, yet loveable sort of way, even though most people might not be aware of it.

Mychal Judge communicated a spirituality that was incarnational and human. His faith was clearly not divorced from his life. His pastoral care continued to be directed toward anyone who was struggling, regardless of whether that person was on a journey in faith or not. Praying for others was a spiritual workout. Brian Purfield remembered walking to the library late in the evening and often passing Mychal in the corridor. He sometimes wondered where Mychal had been, and one night he found out:

> I went into the chapel, and he was kneeling on the step right
> in front of the tabernacle, holding his arms out and spend-

ing time in prayer. I got the impression this was a regular occurrence. That was his recharging, his handing over what had happened during the day into the hands of the Lord. He also had a great devotion to the Virgin Mary. You might have thought he was a party man and had to be around people, but he also needed his time alone, in front of the Blessed Sacrament.

But for all his private piety, Father Judge's public exuberance did not suit the temperament of some of the older, more traditional Franciscans. One of them would walk out of the chapel when he discovered it was Mychal Judge's turn to say Mass. "Some of our old friars found him quite difficult to accept because he was very informal," Father Anthony McNeill explained. "He wouldn't stick to the canon of the Eucharistic Prayer of the Mass. He was very creative with it. He would read it, take it inside himself, and then change it. He would make it more a personal prayer and include people within it. He wouldn't stay with a rigid liturgy. He was the type of man who could not be confined within a system or fixed way of doing things."

While liturgically Mychal Judge was somewhat untraditional, it was clear his homilies were honed from the quarry of his own experience where, said Brian Purfield, there had been "a lot of digging and scraping." Preaching was a means of integrating and making fruitful the pains of the past. He was not a wounded healer who ever doubted the love of others. Even if some fellow Franciscans could not stomach his unconventionality, there were plenty of admirers. Ultimately he was tremendously aware of God's love for him. Everything he had was a gift to him. He would say, "Have whatever you want. Nothing is mine. I'm just so happy that I am alive."

His homilies addressed issues of forgiveness and acceptance: acceptance of oneself and acceptance of others. "No matter what mess you are in, you are still held and loved by God," he would tell his British congregations. Judge's own self-acceptance had manifested an inner freedom that others found threatening. He did not sit on the fence on any issue. AIDS was proving a challenge for the church at the time. While not outspoken on the issue, he did have strong opinions. His concern for those living with HIV and AIDS was authentically compassionate, but the prevailing climate in British Catholic circles was one of suspicion, even condemnation. "He came across at Canterbury as a liberated person, someone happy with his own sexuality, his own person," said Brian Purfield. "In a very British sense, we were a little more reserved and some of the older friars found it very difficult to accept him."

He was a larger-than-life figure. People either liked him or they didn't. He preferred to speak personally about faith in general and his own faith in particular. But he never said anything that could be considered shocking.

Ironically, the person most intolerant of Father Mychal's approach happened to share the same surname. Father Urban Judge was a former English provincial and firmly seated at the other end of the Franciscan spectrum. He had been a canon lawyer and was in poor health. In semi-retirement at Canterbury, he would teach courses on canon law and worked as secretary of the province. According to some friars of the time, Father Urban, who had chosen a name after a pope, "had all the stereotypes you could think of." Mychal Judge seemed "to smash them one after another, even without trying. That was a tremendously dangerous thing to do." The younger Judge was no respecter of titles. He would relate to a beggar in the same way he would a leading religious authority. Common human dignity mattered much more than hierarchical status.

Father Mychal was greatly hurt by Father Urban's attitude toward him. Tensions ran high. A friend commented:

> Father Urban almost could not stand the sight of him. If you were on the same table and the two of them were there, there was a silence. But there was no bridging the gap, even though Mychal tried many times. It was both the fact of his

personality and the fact that he was out as a gay man, but never crusadingly so. It got to the stage where Father Urban could not stay in the same room as Mychal or, if he were forced to, would go off to another corner of it, away from Mychal. It was painful to see. It affected Mychal. It did hurt him. But he would still carry on, and he was never really condemnatory of Father Urban.

MYCHAL JUDGE'S SENSE of theatricality enlivened the more subdued atmosphere of the English house of formation and studies. Students who might otherwise have contributed to the exuberance held back because they were being evaluated. Mychal, once described as being "a bit too loud even for the States," wasn't being assessed and refused to reign himself in.

"I don't think his sexuality was a big issue for him at that time, but it might have been for other people," said Brian Purfield. "It was intuited or assumed by others. He wouldn't deny his sexuality but he wouldn't promote it either. Nonetheless he was very good with a couple of students who were struggling with identity issues, and they found in him somebody who understood them and with whom they could talk. It was clear he was comfortable with his own life."

Mychal's closest friend in Canterbury was another friar, Father Peter Daly, who had been a professional dancer. Like Mychal, he combined a natural zest for life with an ability to reflect prayerfully on the human condition. There was an instant connection and mutual attraction. They lived in the same house and "fed off each other." There was an ongoing camaraderie that appealed to less outgoing students who were nonetheless drawn to both friars. But Father Urban Judge was not sympathetic to any of the humor ignited by their conversations.

FATHER MYCHAL'S LOVE of fun never compromised his underlying sense of pastoral responsibility. Few people knew the lengths he would go to help others. He became chaplain at a U.S. air force base but rarely spoke about his ministry there. "He would never trumpet things," said Brian Purfield. "You would just stumble across them. He used to get many calls from the States from people still wanting his advice and prayers, even though he was out of the country."

But it was the generosity of Mychal Judge that always struck Brian Purfield.

> You would go to his room, and he would say, "Whatever is here you can have." It wasn't a throwaway line. He meant it. He would just go to a drawer and give you whatever you wanted. He'd say, "How are your clothes? You look as though you might be cold on that trip you're making. Take this sweater." It would have been given to him, but it was never his. A gift was always something he shared or gave away. If there were money there, he would just hand you the bills: it was just paper to him. He was never one to hoard things. People would send him money from the States, and he would use it to take some of the friars up to London to see a show. He didn't flaunt his kindness but felt he had to share everything.

Mychal Judge attended meetings of Alcoholics Anonymous in Canterbury. While this did not surprise friends who knew his background, even they were taken aback when he decided to convene an open A.A. meeting at the Franciscan International Study Centre. One of them recalled the risk he was taking:

> In the context of the time, with the former provincial there, drink was something you did not do. If a friar had trouble with drink, it was hushed up or he was sent away for therapy. Alcoholism was one of the worst sins. Suddenly Mychal Judge arrived, openly admitted he had had a drink problem, and then invited everyone to an open A.A. meeting at the formation house of the province. This was unheard of. The nerve he had! But there was this sense of freedom about him.

Although Mychal Judge later dispensed with anonymity, A.A. members tend not to disclose their identities. "Jimmy Guitar," a recovering alcoholic who now earns his living in Kent teaching classical guitar, remembered the Monday night Father Judge turned up at an A.A. meeting in the Quaker Meeting House. Members found him open, bright, and lively. During the course of the year, Mychal made a serious contribution to the group and even became its secretary. There were up to thirty members, men and women. Some were still drinking and having difficulty stopping. Mychal was the only priest at that time. The others included two doctors, businessmen, a retired major, and a number of people off the street who were sleeping in the streets. Mychal gave them particular attention, and they found him easy to be with.

"We knew he was a priest, but he asked us not to address him as 'Father,'" said Jimmy Guitar. "We knew him as Mychal, just another A.A. member. He was very much a recovering alcoholic like the rest of us. But he was different in that he was particularly positive as a person and gave out a lot of joy. He was a good listener, so people could approach him very easily. These qualities were not uncommon in other members, but I felt they were a little more prominent in Mychal."

While Father Mychal did not disclose much about his own suffering, he was able to be a personal friend to many members. His pastoral support to Jimmy Guitar changed Jimmy's life. Jimmy had gone through a difficult patch in sobriety. He had gone through a divorce, sold a business, and found himself homeless and jobless. Jimmy would go to the Franciscan center and talk with Mychal about affirmation, identity, spirituality, and the meaning of God in their lives. Father Mychal supported him on his faith journey. Jimmy's strict Roman Catholic upbringing had created immense hurdles for him in the early stages of recovery, especially his fears of God and the church. Jimmy recalled:

> I found in Father Mychal a wonderful middleman who really put me in touch with my soul. I did in fact move back toward

the church after that. I found it easier to return to the faith I had grown up with. He wasn't the main instrument but he was a big part of it. It was just his being.

There was tremendous warmth and joy that he imparted. On the one occasion I came up to his room and casually mentioned it was my birthday. "Ah," he said. "I have something for you." He opened the cupboard and gave me a lovely brand-new shirt. That was the kind of person he was — generous immediately. I still have the shirt, which I treasure now particularly.

Judith Rosato got to know Mychal through Masses at the center and invited him out to her farm. "On the first occasion," she recalled, "he crossed the threshold saying, 'God bless this house and all who live in it.' Of all of the religious I have ever known connected with the center, none has ever come to the house and said anything like that, before they've even greeted you. That tells you what sort of a man he was."

Mychal relaxed on his visits to the farm. As soon as the weather improved for a barbecue, he would say to Judith: "The forecast's good. Can we have a cookout?" He taught her sons American sport: "Keep your eye on the ball or you'll never be able to play baseball." He was as engaging with children as he was with grownups. At one of the lunches, Judith Rosato offered Father Mychal a glass of wine. He declined and later told her that he had been an alcoholic. He explained: "Every morning I get out of my bed, kneel down, and ask God to help me to get through that day without a drink."

Judith said that Mychal wanted to try to find his feet through a smaller and closer community. She believes this was one of the reasons he was in Canterbury — to renew his faith in his Franciscan family. He once intimated that he thought St. Francis wanted his message carried throughout the world. He was looking to marry his American background with this sense of internationalism. Judith recounted:

He had so much love. It wasn't that you liked Mychal. You loved Mychal because he was one of those people who embraced you. He always had time for you. When he talked to you, he would never look over your shoulder at someone else. You were the most important person in the world at that time. That is a great gift as well. Some people cultivate that gift, but he had it naturally.

He wasn't given the opportunity to say very many Masses, but at the last one he said at the center he got very excited. He asked the whole congregation to hold hands and say the Our Father together. When we had done it, he said: "I have been waiting twelve months to say it together like this."

During his year in Canterbury, Mychal Judge visited Ireland and got to know parts of Europe, including France and the former Nazi concentration camp of Auschwitz in Poland. He also visited London as much as he could. Once he was invited to a graduation at a university. Asked to join the procession, he found a doctoral robe and put it on, joking: "They wouldn't want just a brown habit so I've borrowed this red scarf and hood to put over it."

Although the year was not always as exuberant on the inside as it was on the outside, it was a time for him to break out of conventionality after a lifetime of traditional Franciscanism. The experience changed him. After he had returned to the States, a confrere visiting Canterbury asked the friars: "What *have* you done with Mychal Judge? When he left us, he was a conventional parish priest."

The sabbatical year was one of the reference points in his life. His Franciscan friend Brian Carroll says he loved the year and always talked about it:

Dressing up in denim was not out of character considering who he had been. I think if he saw it was ruffling some feathers, he would ruffle them all the more and have fun doing it. He was a character. If people took themselves — or him — too seriously he would play that up all the more.

I think he was perhaps also trying to make a statement that a Franciscan or a priest is someone who can get out of the sanctuary and change into something comfortable. I think he just wanted a break. He read, but he was not a student. No one assumed Mychal was going to Canterbury to study. It was assumed he was going on vacation. It was a time to travel, see people, and be free.

The English interlude was a watershed in Mychal Judge's life. Returning to New York with greater self-confidence and vision, he set about inaugurating a ministry to the city's latest outcasts. A black cloud had been hovering over New York's gay community. Death and disfigurement overshadowed a world once character-ized by liveliness and beauty. But the church was frightened. Many Catholic priests refused to go anywhere near people living with HIV and AIDS. But a loving Franciscan, inspired by a saint who had touched lepers, would soon be back in town, anointing their heads and massaging their feet.

11

NIGHT VIGILS

———⚬⚬⚬———

S TEVEN J. SMURR was a young and talented New York fashion designer. Charismatic and creative, with dark good looks, he had grown up as a Catholic in Columbus, Ohio, and served an internship with Armani. His work was already highly acclaimed. He was on the verge of stardom. He wanted to be where the party was. People loved being around him. Heads turned when he walked down the street.

Then, in his late twenties, Steven was diagnosed with AIDS. Despite the new treatments, he continued to get infections and had to give up the work he loved. Like many others at that time, he even had to bring a lawsuit against his employers and insurance companies because of their reluctance to compensate people with HIV and AIDS — even though they had dutifully paid the premiums. Steven had lost many friends to AIDS through death. Others deserted him when they discovered that he too had the virus.

Steven became involved with the city's Dignity/AIDS ministry. There he met Michael Mulligan, and the two became lovers. Their relationship lasted until Steven's death less than two years later. Michael Mulligan had to witness his partner's diminishment. "That was a struggle," he said. "On many occasions we fought the good fight and found ways to ease some of the pain." There was a point where Steven could no longer eat. Attending meetings at the Gay Men's Health Crisis, where he was updated on new treatments, he discovered a dental cream to numb the back of his throat. That was the only way Steven could get nutrition into his fragile body. New drugs made him nauseous and caused him to vomit.

Disfigured through the illness, Steven also became so emaciated that, if he rolled the wrong way, he would bruise. To soothe the pain and discomfort, Michael would fill the tub with bubble bath and gently bathe him in the warm water.

Michael Mulligan was already a friend of Mychal Judge, and Steven knew him through the Dignity Masses. Steven became enamored of the priest. "He thought Mychal was one of the greatest human beings he could have met," Mulligan recalled.

> After his visits, Steven would say he was an incredible person. Steven saw Jesus in Mychal but could become bashful about it. He knew Mychal was gay and that was how they connected. Sometimes Mychal would even say things that would make Steven blush. He became a presence for Steven. In that respect he had Mychal as a priest and a confidant, but also as a gay friend. He could talk to him about me and how I would handle things after he died. Father Mychal accompanied Steven to the portal of death.

Steven became so close to Mychal Judge that he was able to ask him to comfort his mother and father. He was always in touch with his family and told his parents of "this wonderful Father Mike" in his life.

Mychal Judge was also a buttress for Michael Mulligan during his months of caring for Steven. "I saw in him an incredible amount of strength and trust. He always said, 'It's gonna be okay. It's gonna be okay.' Then he put a father-like arm around me."

In the fall of 1989, Steven suffered appendicitis and, after surgery, Michael feared his partner would give up. But eventually he started walking again and, for the next few weeks, the sun shone. Then Steven caught another infection and began to experience problems with his lungs. Again he improved but needed further treatment. In November, Steven was taken back into the hospital. Michael knew he would not return home. They urged the doctors to try any new treatments. For a while steroids appeared to ease the breathing difficulties, but his lungs kept collapsing.

On the evening of November 21, Michael started to worry that his partner would not pull through this time, so he called Mychal Judge. The priest rushed over and a night-long vigil began. They talked to Steven and prayed over him. Mychal would say: "Listen, it's all in God's hands. Don't worry. It's going to be okay. It's going to be okay." They discussed increasing the number of steroids to seal up the punctured lung but Steven had clearly had enough. "I wasn't ready to let him go. It was Father Mychal who said, 'Relax. You'll just have to trust.' Thank goodness Mychal was there. We spent the entire night in the hospital."

While Steven was still conscious, Father Mychal anointed him with sacred oil, a ritual that used to be known as the last rites: "I had the medical power to tell the doctors to try another operation or to let him go," said Michael. "During the vigil he was quite conscious, although he was starting to go out of it. We kept saying to him, 'You can't go until your mom and dad and sisters get here.' He must have heard it because he hung on like a trooper until they arrived the next morning."

Not knowing for certain when Steven would die, Father Mychal left the ward because of other pastoral commitments. Surrounded by Steven's family later that afternoon, the eve of Thanksgiving, Michael Mulligan watched his lover depart: "It was a most incredible moment to witness — to watch Steven pull in the last breath of life and turn over. Then his head dropped."

Father Mychal conducted Steven Smurr's funeral in New York and then boarded a plane with Michael Mulligan and accompanied the body on its journey back to Ohio. There he led a second funeral for all Steven's family and friends in Columbus. Such poignant services were replicated many times in different settings.

THE FIRST OUTBREAK of AIDS in New York had occurred in the early 1980s. Mychal Judge was pertinently aware that the city had witnessed the decimation of an entire generation of gay men in their early twenties and thirties by what was originally known as GRID: Gay Related Immune Deficiency. Person after person had fallen prey to an unknown, misunderstood, and ignominious disease. Six hundred of those who attended the Dignity Masses regularly at Saint Francis Xavier in Greenwich Village died in less than ten years. Father Bernard Lynch had organized the first AIDS ministry in the city in 1982 and had been brought on to the newly formed mayor's task force on AIDS. People with the virus were both feared and ostracized in ways that are today inconceivable. There was no HIV test. People got sick and died.

Gay people in New York all thought that they had the virus because there was then no way of knowing how it was contracted. Fear and paranoia cohabited. Those working among people with AIDS spent more time changing bedsheets and making diapers for their friends than they did trying to make sense of what was happening. Hospital orderlies and nurses refused to take food to HIV patients in their sick rooms fearing that they would "catch it." There were even accounts of HIV patients found starving by their loved ones when they came to visit. Churches, synagogues, and funeral homes closed their doors for the same reasons. Camus's plague was reality. Bernard Lynch reflected:

> We took bodies from hospitals to crematoriums. More ashes went into the Hudson River at Christopher Street in Greenwich Village than I care to remember. We drank from our own wells, and the water was blood. Along with many other priests and some religious brothers, Mychal Judge and I were only too conscious of how particularly painful and extraordinarily difficult it was for those of our profession who had been diagnosed HIV-positive. At the beginning of the pandemic all hell broke loose in denial and cover-up by the archdiocese and religious orders. With time a frosty kind of tolerance prevailed and HIV-positive priests and religious were "supported" on condition that they would remain absolutely silent.

On his return from England, Mychal Judge inaugurated the
St. Francis AIDS ministry on Thirty-first Street, which mobilized
money, resources, and people to care for men and women in the
first wave of the AIDS epidemic. The work harmonized his pastoral
gifts, his ability to be present to people, his understanding of healing through prayer and the sacraments, his capacity for publicity,
and his fund-raising skills. It was an opportunity to integrate his
Franciscan spirit, his priesthood, and his sexuality into a ministry of
compassion. After the difficulties between Dignity and the church,
he had to adjust his thinking about how he would represent himself
in relationship to the gay life and the moral issues it raised. He knew
he had to work within the institution, and he was fully aware of
the challenges. He distanced himself from Dignity and was not the
visible presence at meetings Bernard Lynch had been. Nonetheless,
he became a bridge between the church and the gay community at
a time when both sides were mutually suspicious. He followed the
Franciscan ideal of "loving the leper within" so his external compassion for others was never tainted by fear or any hint of prejudice.

No other parish was willing to risk developing an AIDS ministry, especially among drug addicts. Few priests would take
funerals; even fewer undertakers would handle the bodies. Relationships between the Catholic Church and the gay community
were so damaged that few gay Catholics dared even ask for the
sacraments. Bill Hacdrich, who assisted Mychal Judge and then
directed the AIDS ministry project, explained that the church's
presence with gay men was nothing short of divisive. But a lot
of families called and wanted Father Mychal to visit. He dedicated himself to caring for those who were sick and their partners
and relatives. Those living with HIV and AIDS also had spiritual
needs in trying to understand their suffering in the context of
their relationship with God. In many ways they were faced with a
new identity crisis: they wanted to know who they were as human
beings, as gay people confronting death.

Mychal Judge became involved in his busy routine of going
into hospitals, liaising with social workers, visiting people's apart-

ments — and taking funerals. Word soon got around and people started to seek him out. Bill Haedrich felt he was overextended because of his inability to turn anyone down. Most of their clients lived in single rooms in the city. Father Mychal was one of the few priests of the time who would visit them at home. Those who answered the door were often drug addicts.

Where people were feeling small or frightened, he seems to have had a particular capacity for recognizing their insecurities without causing embarrassment. This gift personalized his ministry and enabled him to be "amazingly salvific," as one person put it. He was never fully aware of the extent to which his pastoral sensitivity improved other people's sense of self-esteem. The wound of his own self-questioning was healing incognito.

But Mychal Judge and Bill Haedrich did not disguise the nature of their work. They advertised and had cards printed. One day they might give a radio interview, the next give a talk to a curious parish. Their outreach was not restricted to Catholics: they took care of any person who rang the bell. Their gifts complemented each other. Bill was the meticulous administrator, dealing with day-to-day organization. Mychal had the charisma of connecting with people and keeping his sights set on the wider frame.

> You knew he was being drained. He had all that energy from having stopped his drinking. He would go on into the night. There was a well that could not be satisfied by anybody. You could be with him and spend hours with him. But there was still more he wanted. He would often say to people "Have you seen God?" This underlay his spiritual and religious understanding. He was almost mystical. There was some depth in him that could not be reached by others — or even himself possibly.

Bill Haedrich said he got on with Father Mychal "for the most part." The priest was Irish and loved a good "fight." They would often banter back and forth. "We could argue about an issue lightly. We were both very direct. He liked a fight with someone who had good energy. Once I remember fighting with him, and he came down later and apologized. We hugged and we were both sorry that we got angry with each other."

Tom Ferriter remembered visiting him on Thirty-first Street and trying to persuade him to go and have lunch. "It was a big deal to drag him out for a sandwich. He just didn't eat." Suddenly, Mychal Judge emerged from a small room and asked if Tom could wait. Later he came out with an Irish American woman and her young daughter — all three were crying. After they left, Mychal asked for time to compose himself. He then told Tom that he had needed to explain to them that the woman's son and her daughter's brother had AIDS. "I've done too much of that lately," he added.

Father Mychal was visiting St. Clare's and St. Vincent's, two Catholic hospitals that specialized in caring for AIDS patients. Often he would hold the hand of patients and tell them quietly that he understood something of their journey because he too was gay. He spoke gently as he anointed their ears, eyes, hands, and feet. Their feelings of rejection were acute — not even dentists would see them. Mychal Judge not only went close. He touched. He took in teddy bears and stuffed animals, signs of unconditional love, a ministry that helped many gay people, alienated from the church, reconnect with their faith. Father Mychal was a living symbol of the church as it ought to be. "If it wasn't for the Mychals of this world, I don't know what would have happened," commented one helper, Tom Patterson, who had by then become disillusioned with the Catholic Church. "I told him the church was driving me crazy. When I had finished, Mychal said he wanted to recite a short Protestant hymn he had learned in England: 'Jesus, Jesus, this I know, 'cause the Bible tells me so. Yes, Jesus loves me, yes, Jesus loves me.' He told me that if I believed that, I would never get mad at anybody." Once Mychal Judge came back from Japan and presented Tom Patterson with a little Buddha statue. He told him: "If you get all crazy or out of your mind, as you usually do, just look at the statue of the Buddha and meditate. You will feel like a million dollars." Tom asked what had happened to Christ. Mychal answered: "He belongs here too, but Buddha doesn't do a bad job."

FATHER JOHN J. MCNEILL, a Jesuit for nearly forty years before being expelled from the Society of Jesus in 1987 for his public stance on gay and lesbian ministry, was Mychal Judge's spiritual director for a time. McNeill, who got to know Judge through his AIDS ministry, said the Franciscan was such an extraordinary person that people would naturally gravitate to him. He radiated love. If he knew anybody who was down and out, he had to bring God's love to that person:

> He once told me that frequently when he would go into the room of AIDS patients wearing his Franciscan robes, he would run into real hostility from those who had been badly burned by the church — and that would be most. He tried to figure out how to bring them God's message without preaching because he knew that was unacceptable to them. He came up with what he thought was a brilliant idea. He would go into their rooms and, despite the state of the patients' bodies, would pull back the blankets and massage their feet. That was his approach. People were afraid to be in the room with them or even talk with them. But here was this very gentle and wonderful person coming in and massaging their feet. That would break down all their resistance! It did take courage because there was a real fear.

McNeill, author of the controversial book *The Church and the Homosexual*, told me that Judge had communicated a deep spirituality to everyone by his extraordinary joy and loving spirit. When you met him, he looked at you and smiled. "For those of us who were aware, we knew we were dealing with somebody who was directly in line with God. He was a very special presence." McNeill said "the sure sign" of genuine sanctity was for one to be totally present in the here and now with the person one was dealing with.

Mychal Judge had that ability to an extraordinary degree. It was a total, unlimited, and unconditional presence.

God uses wounded healers, and it was precisely because of what he had been through that he achieved that extraordinary degree of union with the divine. Brokenness cannot be healed by people who haven't experienced it. I think he was a modern-day mystic because the essence of mysticism is the spirit of love.

New York state senator Tom Duane, himself HIV positive, first met Father Judge at the funerals of friends. He was often the priest who would say the funeral Mass. In the early days, Duane never heard of him ever turning down a request of a family or a lover to perform a funeral Mass. Not every Catholic church wanted to celebrate Masses for people with AIDS. Not every family was accepting of their children dying of AIDS. He always said the right things at the funerals.

I spent a lot of the 1980s and the 1990s thinking I was going to die soon and wondering why I hadn't. I had often thought I would want Father Mychal Judge to say my funeral Mass because I thought he would be a great comfort to my family. It's sad and ironic that he died before I did. I've now lived long enough to have to try to find someone to match the spirituality and the sense of humor and the sensitivity of Mychal Judge. I am going to have to find someone else. I don't even know where to start to look because he was just the clear choice for me. If we're looking for saintly people in New York City, he would certainly fit the bill.

Debi Rabbene, who lost three brothers to AIDS in two years, told me how Father Mychal Judge had entered her life after she had encountered prejudice from doctors, nurses, funeral homes, and the church itself. Even neighbors would walk away when she told them the cause of her gay brothers' deaths.

After Arthur, forty, and Willi, thirty-one, died in 1991, the family felt it important to validate their lives through a memorial Mass in their home. Many friends were devastated, and the family themselves needed closure. Debi's brother John, who had himself been diagnosed with AIDS, knew he would be the next to die. He agreed to find a priest to take the service, but was unable to persuade any. The clergy were either too afraid or too busy. The family was determined that the memorial would go ahead even if they had to conduct it themselves. Even on the morning of the service, a willing priest was still proving elusive. Then, unexpectedly, they learned that Father Mychal Judge had been told of their dilemma and would be delighted to oblige. At short notice, he would drive the thirty miles to Bethpage on Long Island where they lived. "We had put up with abuse, and then he came," said Debi.

> It was like we had always known him. He had such empathy for all of us and was so in tune. We were hurting so badly. He could not believe what we had gone through. We had people wall-to-wall and he worked the room. He put everybody at ease. After the Mass, he comforted my mother and then went over to my brother John. After that day, John was at ease with his illness and felt he could go on. At the end of the service, Father Mychal asked people to sing "God Bless America." His mother had once said to him: "If you don't know what else to do, sing a song." One woman, who went to church several times a week, said she had never been to a service that had touched her so much.

Willi had asked that his remains be buried in Florida, but Arthur's ashes had been buried in his sister's garden. Father Mychal agreed to bless the burial ground and the shrubs. Never once did he mention that Arthur and Willi had died of AIDS or had been gay. The memorial had been about love and pain. It did not matter what other people thought because these were two brothers who had been deeply loved. "When he left, Father

Mychal actually thanked us for letting him come and share the time with us," said Debi.

He made us feel he was equal with us, not better than us. We felt a lot of priests would look down on us and not approve. But he helped us bring out the fact that we loved our brothers, that they had passed away, and that we missed them. I was losing my faith, not in God, but in the church, because it wasn't there when I needed it. Mychal Judge did not make my faith in God stronger, but he made me believe in the Catholic Church more. He inspired me to minister. He was there when we needed him, so I have decided I will now be there for others when they need me.

These were the words Mychal Judge spoke that day:

Sometimes in life when we lose someone we love and we don't know what to do, we should just pray and worship. Thank you Lord for their lives, for their love, creativity, for their friendship; their good days and bad, for their happiness, for their anger; for everything they brought into our lives. These are things we should say about each other, always. If we did, life wouldn't be half bad. I hope some day that someone says things nicely about me as I said about them through the years. I love you, so just love each other. The best you can.

Father William Hart McNichols, a Jesuit priest and Third Order Franciscan who supported Mychal Judge's AIDS ministry, told me that all this showed that Father Mychal had the charism, or spiritual gift, of the wounds of St. Francis. People did not see a divided person. As a priest who was gay he belonged to the group that bore the wounds of the church.

Mychal Judge took the charism of the wounds into the world in terms of his sexuality. In many respects he lived a very open life as a gay Catholic priest, attending meetings of Dignity, regularly joining gay gatherings of A.A., and supporting gay friends publicly. But he never trumpeted the fact he was gay or politicized it. Despite all his internal battles with faith and sexuality, he was able to be alongside people on their comfort level. He was never psychologically troubled or socially awkward in the company of others because he was a gay man. "And that," Father McNichols suggested, "was the source of his tremendous strength. He was always warm and friendly. He never came across as someone completely together, but he projected a wounded warmth without being wounding. A lot of ministers, who are not self-aware or self-conscious in the good sense of that word, can really hurt people because their wounds are not absorbed or faced. They can really damage others. When Mychal Judge came toward you, you knew he was wounded. But you also knew you were safe with him."

12

"BLESSED ARE
THE PERSECUTED"

_{⸺ ∞ ⸺}

I N 1986 a Vatican statement on homosexuality alienated gay and lesbian Catholics even further from the church. The nine-page *Letter to the Bishops of the Catholic Church on the Pastoral Care of Homosexual Persons* laid out specific guidelines for the spiritual lives of gay and lesbian people. The announcement from the Congregation for the Doctrine of the Faith stated unequivocally: "Although the particular inclination of the homosexual is not a sin, it is more or less a strong tendency ordered toward an intrinsic moral evil; and thus the inclination itself must be seen as an objective disorder."

Father Bernard Lynch, who had founded the Dignity AIDS ministry several years earlier, endorsed the stance taken by Father John McNeill, who had spoken out publicly against the letter. Father Lynch, a member of the Society of African Missions, was ordered by his superiors to take a sabbatical in Rome "to recuperate."

The statement from Rome dealt a strong blow to Dignity's status within the church. Following its publication, several bishops refused to allow its chapters to use churches and other diocesan property for liturgies and meetings. Despite negotiations with the New York chancery, the group was forced to leave St. Francis Xavier Church. Mychal Judge continued to support the organization but, unlike Father Lynch, had no intention of putting his own priesthood on the line. Bernard Lynch was the only Roman Catholic priest to testify before the city council for the successful passage in 1986 of civil-rights legislation for the gay community.

"Mychal Judge was one of the people who said he could not do that and would not do that," Bernard Lynch told me. "I remember Mychal, with tears in his eyes, saying 'Bernard, I admire you. I cannot go with you. But I will support you.'"

When Dignity was finally expelled and had no home, Mychal Judge suggested that the AIDS ministry meet at his own church, and he would act as facilitator. It was important, said Bernard Lynch, for the group to meet on Catholic ground "to give us some sort of Bethlehem where we could belong." Between thirty and seventy people with AIDS-related illnesses attended these weekly retreats. Under this new roof, they were able to deal with such spiritual issues as pain, dying, death, hope for new life, and God's love.

It was Mychal who provided us with a space within which we could meet and deal with these issues through small groups, one-to-ones, prayer, liturgy, discussion. It was so important to have the space in a Catholic church where we could meet and celebrate Eucharist for people with AIDS. He would drop in, but he would leave my job to me. He did not become effectively involved in Dignity at that time other than making sure we had everything we needed.

Mychal Judge took over Father Lynch's AIDS ministry when he left for Rome in June 1987 but did not lose touch with his friend, who was soon to become the focus of international media attention. Father Lynch had ministered to the Catholic gay community in New York since 1977 and had become Dignity's theological consultant. His work with AIDS had incurred severe censure, while his attempts to explain homosexual relationships as acceptable and loving were at odds with the teaching of the church, provoking bitter conflict with Cardinal O'Connor. Then, in May 1988, Father Lynch, who was working as a high-school chaplain and counselor in the Bronx, was charged on five counts of child abuse following false accusations from a fourteen-year-old pupil.

Bernard Lynch's recollections of the time highlighted the heroic lengths Mychal Judge would go to in his care for others, even when his own reputation was at stake. After his spell in Rome, Father Lynch had gone back to his native Ireland, trying to discern his future. It was then that he had received word that the FBI was looking for him and intended to press serious charges. "I collapsed into total, utter, absolute incredulous despair," Bernard Lynch recalled.

All I could see was my being crucified on the cross literally and wishing with all my heart I would die quickly. I was under house arrest. As the story broke sensationally in the media in Ireland and America, I had a phone call from Mychal Judge, who agreed to come over to Ireland. When he arrived, he was very warm as always. He put his arms around me, kissed me on the cheek, and cried because I was in bits. He was using words like "bastards" and at the same time saying, "Bernard, don't be surprised. They did the same to Jesus."

At the time, Lynch's provincial, Father Cornelius Murphy, and his advisors were prevaricating on whether or not to pay his defense bill. After all, Lynch had not worked directly for his order since he had taken up an assignment for the archdiocese. They knew the costs would be extortionate because he would be cross-examined by a top prosecuting attorney. Enquiries indicated Lynch was about to be made an example to any priest who might think of standing up for the gay cause. Lynch explained:

The order was playing it safe, so Mychal Judge insisted on meeting my provincial. Afterward he told me his task was to inform and "flesh out" for the provincial the truth of what was really happening in the archdiocese. Before leaving the States, Mychal Judge, along with a number of leading Jesuits and Dominicans, had tried to make contact with officials in the church, but they were completely stonewalled.

At the end of his conversations with Mychal Judge, my provincial went to the media, made his first public statement about me, and released whatever funds necessary. Not one penny would be spared. Mychal Judge was one of several priests who, with my order, saved the day — and probably my life. There is no doubt I would have got fifteen years in jail. Everything was against me: the Catholic Church, the New York archdiocese — one of the most powerful in the world — and the FBI.

I did not realize that Mychal Judge had played such an important role. I literally did not know at the time what time of the day it was. I cannot exaggerate how totally broken I was. His caring was also very spiritual in the sense that he was able to talk me through the gospel and show what was happening to me. Although I found it very hard to hear, it was consoling. He drew on the accounts of the Crucifixion in terms of my innocence and on the words of Jesus, "The truth shall set you free." He quoted the very beautiful line from St. Matthew's Gospel, "Blessed are those who suffer persecution for justice' sake." He came to the private oratory of the priest I was staying with, Father Laurence Wrenne, and prayed with me. I remember kneeling down and asking him to give me his blessing. It was very emotional because he was crying, and I was in bits.

Even though Mychal Judge succeeded in doing as much as he could, there was no guarantee, even with the best defense, that Father Lynch would get off. Father Mychal was under no illusion. Shocked by the publicity the case received in Ireland, he said he hadn't realized how anticlerical its media could be. "I looked like a terrorist. I was being brought out in dark sunglasses and a balaclava, so people wouldn't recognize me," Father Lynch explained. Characteristically, Mychal Judge asked Bernard Lynch how his family was coping. He even offered to drive eighty miles to Ennis in County Clare to visit his father. Over tea and slices

of apple tart, they chatted for several hours. The father later told
his son:

> It meant so much to me to have a priest come, confirm that
> you were innocent, tell me about the politics in New York
> and how politically involved the church was there. Every-
> body knew about what was going on, but only two people
> came to see me — and one of them was Mychal Judge. He
> was the first one with which I had a conversation. I was
> brokenhearted and did not know what was going to happen.
> Everybody in the town was talking about us.

When Father Lynch returned to New York, Father Mychal
became a key member of what was called "the blue ribbon coalition" of priests who met with Lynch's attorney, Michael Kennedy,
and offered advice. Throughout the year-long trial, Mychal Judge
personally attended the packed court hearings in his habit and
solicited others to go and do likewise. "He was there a lot,"
recalled Father Lynch. "If I didn't see him, I missed him. He was
there that often. He would just come up to me, put his arms
around me, and say, 'How you doing, guy? You're going to get
through. You're going to get through.' He was very physical and
very affectionate. He had no inhibitions about being demonstra-
tive, which was very unusual for Irish American Catholics. He
was a very obvious presence and would telephone me. He was
doing all the giving."

In April 1989, after "a trial of my very soul," Father Lynch was
cleared. The prosecution case collapsed as it became apparent
the evidence against him had been fabricated. "On that day of
the exoneration and declaration of innocence Mychal Judge was
so jubilant. He cried, but they were tears of joy."

The friendship between the two priests developed and, although
they did not always agree, they conversed spiritedly about the
church and politics. Mychal Judge would always differentiate
between the church as the people of God and the church as an institution. He saw his mission as being very much "a people's priest."

He told Bernard Lynch that he did not understand the church's problem with homosexuality. "He used to be totally amazed that the church was making an issue of how people loved each other. One of his great lines was, 'Is there so much love in the world that we can afford to discriminate against any kind of love?' "

There was a great sense of camaraderie when you were in Mychal Judge's company. A tactile man of great affectivity, he incarnated his own spirit and lived in his own body. His struggle with his sexuality was external. It concerned what the Roman Catholic Church taught and, as a consequence, what society expected. "It wasn't at all Mychal Judge's problem," Lynch argued.

> He didn't make it his problem. He stepped into another realm in terms of his relationship to God in Christ. He was a deeply mystical person but, while he was devout at Mass and in his celebration of it, he was able to carry that same devotedness into his relationships with people. He did see himself as the Body of Christ and he saw others as that, as truly as he saw the Eucharist as the Body of Christ. He saw the institutional church's attitude to the body as the antithesis of the gospel, and he proved that in the way he lived and the way he loved. He was a very incarnational person in the way he looked at you, in the way he smiled, and the way he touched.

Father Lynch said people knew Judge as a man of prayer, not because of any personal piety, but because of the depth of his humanity. It was evident he had suffered. He could appreciate another person's pain without needing to talk excessively. He would nod his head and look someone directly in the face. "I knew this man had been where I was, even though it was a different experience of pain," said Bernard Lynch. "Mychal's greatest commandment to me was, 'Thou Shalt Not Bullshit.' But he was not politically naïve. He knew when to be quiet. He knew how to play the system, and he certainly played it in my favor."

Mychal Judge was self-revelatory. He did not perform ministry. He shared himself — "very honestly, very openly, maybe too much. He had a tangible presence, which was easily missed. He believed very much in the sacramental Real Presence, but he himself had that as well. Whether laughing, joking, or talking, there was a real presence in what he said. He was anything but proud. There was not one conceited bone in his body. His utter ordinariness shone through."

In 1992 Father Lynch's only surviving relative on his father's side died in the Bronx. He said he was expressly forbidden by the archdiocese to celebrate her funeral Mass because of his gay/AIDS activism. But Mychal Judge came to the rescue, presided at the Mass in St. Francis Church, and invited him to preach and concelebrate. This went explicitly against the wishes of the archdiocese. Four years later, when Father Lynch was allowed to celebrate twenty-five years as a priest of the Society of African Missions at St. Paul's Chapel, Columbia University, Mychal Judge hosted all his ordained out-of-town friends to bed and board in the friary. Father Lynch commented: "His friendship for me was the face of God."

13

ON THE EDGE OF THE DEEP

Once when Francis was asked by a poor man for something and he had nothing at hand, he unsewed the border of his tunic and gave it to the poor man. Such was his compassion and such the sincerity with which he followed in the footsteps of the poor Christ.

S O REPORTED Thomas of Celano in *The Second Life of St. Francis*. It might seem a chivalrous tale from the pages of medieval hagiography. But it could just have easily sprung from the twentieth-century exploits of Father Mychal Judge, who treated beggars as friends and made a point of stating that "the filling and emptying of the clothes closet for the homeless" was a dimension of his "grace-filled" Franciscan priesthood.

Mychal Judge's ministry flowered on the margins. He hovered between earth and heaven, life and death, institutional religion and Christian spirituality. He pointed people beyond their own preoccupations. In this sense he was literally eccentric: he moved away from the center or, more accurately, his own comfort. Father Bernard Lynch said he wasn't eccentric in the sense of being odd or absent-minded, for he was always so focused — but eccentric to the extent that he could never hold on to anything. He gave away everything he owned.

Tom Ferriter once called on the friar and noticed a CD player in his room. Knowing he liked Irish music, Tom went out and bought him a batch of discs: "When I returned, the CD player was gone. He had already given the CD player away." He re-donated everything he was given. No matter how much care and originality had gone into choosing a sweater for him, it was likely to end up on somebody else's body. He was excessively careful not to spend money on himself. He would rather walk the streets giving away dollar bills to anyone in need.

Brian Carroll said Mychal's financial scrupulousness and anxiety came from a conviction that from those to whom much had been given, much would be expected. "If someone gave him ten dollars, he would give it away. You had to talk him into spending money on himself. He had an appetite for travel so you could twist his arm and get him to spend the money on that. But there was some anxiety over it."

His attitudes were clearly shaped by a spirituality of subtraction. While unstinting in his desire to give totally, the manner in which Judge passed on gifts suggests he was obsessive about not being obsessive — as far as materialism went. St. Francis felt that to have possessions was to be possessed by them, but Mychal Judge's inability to hold on to things for long seems to have been distinctly psychological. The act of handing over or ridding himself of something he had been invited to own was generous and cathartic at the same time. His attitude to ministry spanned the spectrum, uniting aspects of Catholic guilt with manifestations of the Protestant work ethic. He would tell friars who turned to him for advice: "Get out all day, do your work. Serve the people and minister to them, break your ass, then come back and rest. This is your task, your ministry."

MYCHAL JUDGE had long been influenced by the Franciscan presence in New York. On Black Tuesday, October 29, 1929, the stock market crashed and the Great Depression gripped the city, creating hunger, homelessness, and hopelessness on an unprecedented scale. Brother Gabriel Mehler, a friar at St. Francis Church, knew that if people were going to get through the hard times, they would need "to lean on each other." St. Francis of Assisi had taught others to love the neglected, to feed the hungry, and to care for those who had fallen through the cracks of society. So

Brother Gabriel founded the St. Francis Breadline to help those who could not help themselves. During the worst days of the Depression, it served more than four thousand men and women every morning. The friars haven't missed a morning since. What started out as an emergency charity program to prevent starvation is still operating today, feeding a hundred thousand people a year. Every day at 7:00 A.M. friars walk out on to the sidewalk to feed the hungry women and men of New York City with two simple sandwiches and a cup of coffee. Millions have received food, clothes, and financial assistance over the years. The friars point out that, even in the best of times, people can lose their jobs, children become ill, and houses burn down: "It doesn't matter why people come to us," they say. "It doesn't matter who they are, where they live, or what they do after they get their meals and move on. What matters is that, for one brief moment every day, someone reminds them that they have worth, that they are loved."

Brother Gabriel, known as "The Angel of the Breadline," died in 1940 after serving more than two million people. This example of Franciscan service proved inspirational to a young boy from Brooklyn who, fifty years later, still felt called to serve others, making them aware of their own goodness and worth. The area in front of the church sometimes resembled Penn Station as the poor emerged from the neighboring streets. Some could be heard calling, "Father Mychal, Father Mychal, Father Mychal." One of these friends fought his way up the church's crowded front steps on the day of the priest's funeral Mass to ensure he could pay his respects.

Charlie Galanaugh remembered turning up at the friary to take Father Mychal to dinner, followed by a show. Father Mychal came out to the car and asked: "Do you mind waiting about ten minutes or so? I have to go and check on Howard. He sleeps in that alleyway over there. I just want to check and see if he is all right." Galanaugh offered to go with him but Father Mychal said he would be a little embarrassed if there were someone else there.

He was certain he would be safe. He went off and came back in a few minutes, saying he had to slip into the friary. Galanaugh recalled:

He had discovered that the man was sleeping between buildings. Mychal had given him a big coat because it was rather cold. But somebody had stolen it from him. Mychal came back out with a blanket. It was probably his blanket. He went down the street with it in his arms and came back to the car and said, "I think he'll be all right now. He refuses to come into the house, but he'll be all right." Mychal was the kind of guy to whom you'd say: "You gave him your blanket?" and he would reply: "Well, I don't need it right now. We're on our way to the movies." He reveled in giving away whatever he had. He lived by that poverty rule. He felt that everything he had was God's gift to him and could be given to someone else.

Father Mychal kept money in what he called his "fire truck." He would wind down the window and give money to the beggar squatting at the side of the road, followed by a blessing. Father Anthony McNeill recalled one New Year's Eve in Times Square:

A lot of police officers came up that night and asked him to bless their families and their work. If you were sincere and you asked him for something, he would do his best for you, even getting tickets for people to come over for the St. Patrick's Parade. He might have got a stipend from the fire department and people were generous to him, but he never hung on to things. In his room at the friary, he would pull out a sweater for you and give it away. He wanted to share his blessings and his love and what he had received from God.

But Father McNeill also noted that Mychal Judge had his own credit cards.

And he didn't have *il poverello*, the little poor man, printed on them. He was a more contemporary figure. He liked a good time, but he was modest. He didn't overdress or spend a lot of money on clothes because people gave them to him. He spent money on what mattered — and that was people.

Among Mychal Judge's many roles in New York was that of a board director for Create Incorporated in Central Harlem, a non-sectarian program run by a Franciscan, Father Benedict Taylor. In some ways the project was an extension of the breadline, serving people with alcohol and drug problems, the homeless, senior citizens, single parents, and the hungry. Many were African American or Hispanic. They came from a variety of religious backgrounds, including Catholic, Protestant, and Muslim. Some had been in state and city institutions, including prison. Father Mychal would dutifully bring food and clothing for them. He felt a particular empathy for those with drink addictions, said Father Taylor:

> The people were very poor and were on low incomes — sometimes they were living below the poverty level. Mychal loved it here. He often came in his habit and would arrive in his chaplain's car with the red light and siren. He liked to put all that on as a joke. It was an extension of his humor for our residents. He would sit in on the residents' groups and share his story and then go back out to his car. They would watch him from the step putting on the flashing lights and siren again. It cheered them up. He had a great sense of humor.

He empathized with their troubles. He understood them. They had no need to worry. Each resident was as good a human being as he was. There was hope around for everyone. The hard knocks they had suffered should not dent their confidence. They should go forward. They were as much a part of New York City as he was. He even paid rent for an undocumented person from Trinidad who had AIDS and, according to one friend, "treated him like the mayor of Dublin."

Hospital visiting was also ministry at the margins. When a Hollywood legend lay dying in a New York hospital, he managed to obtain privileged access to her hospital room. He felt hugely proud that he could bring prayer to an icon of the golden age of movies who had become a frail old woman. It was certainly a variation on the Franciscan theme of praising God through the stars.

But his visits to the sick were always authentic. One pal was disappointed when Father Mychal turned down an invitation to spend Christmas with his family. Some weeks later when the friend inquired how he had spent the festive season, Mychal answered: "I visited seven hospitals." The visits were as important to him as they were to the patients. An inability to decline pastoral requests may have been directly connected with a striving for perfection and a lingering doubt about his own self-worth. In any case, Christmas was a time for giving, not receiving. He once famously said: "You know what I want for Christmas? You know what I *really* want? Absolutely nothing! I have everything in the world." It was an attitude that underpinned his philosophy of life.

In his work on the margins, Mychal Judge, who was always intensely patriotic, forged a particularly close relationship with David Dinkins, who became the city's first black mayor. Dinkins told me:

New York owes him a lot — big time. The world owes him a lot. He was a very special human being, irrespective of race, ethnicity, or religion. He used to call by our home unannounced. He would not ask to see us but would just leave an envelope containing a one-page letter. It was really a prayer wishing us well — Easter, Thanksgiving, Christmas, and at other times. He was not a politician and did not involve himself in politics, but he was always comforting, assuring, and helpful.

Dinkins said that Father Judge had made a tremendous contribution because he believed in and was fond of all people. He took them as he found them. He used to say: "See what you can do for others." He was never overbearing. You would not feel that, in his presence, you had to be particularly reverent, stilted, or religious.

New York attorney Brian O'Dwyer, chairman of the Emerald Isle Immigration Center, had equal words of praise. When he had needed help for immigrants and spiritual sustenance for men in the services, he had called on Father Mychal. He was always there to help the people; Irish and Latino immigrants sought and received his guidance. He was an inspiration and never turned anyone down.

> He understood displacement. Being of an Irish American background, he was in the finest tradition of our people in understanding what immigration was about, what being the underdog was all about, what being a person in need of help was all about.

Well-versed in producing sophisticated, clericalized language when required, Mychal Judge could also revel in the language of the street. He knew its shades and color. As he walked back to the friary one night along the streets around the Empire State Building, a dark, bulky figure detached himself from the shadows. It was a gentleman of the road. Menacingly, he approached Mychal Judge and his friend Stephen Weaver. "I was very apprehensive and nervous, but Mychal just waited for him to approach," Weaver recalled. The man said: "Hi, Father Mike, how you doing?" Mychal replied: "I'm good, Harry. How are you?" Harry pointed a finger at Weaver, who was not then ordained, and stabbed his finger toward his chest. "Are you a priest?" Weaver looked to Father Mike for guidance. He nodded, so Weaver said yes. The hobo piped up: "Okay, bless me." Weaver glanced at Judge, who nodded again. Weaver blessed the man, who turned to Judge and commented: "Who's your friend, Mychal? He's okay."

Weaver explained that while Mychal Judge was much at home with the street people of New York, he was also adept at mixing with the more influential — and feeling at home among them too. Father Mychal remembered Washington's Pennsylvania Avenue being "such a simple street" back in 1959 when, as a student, he had watched Charles de Gaulle shaking the hand of President Eisenhower. In the fall of 1962, he even went inside the White House at the invitation of President John F. Kennedy, who received a delegation of Catholic youth leaders. He used to boast about his political connections — but always with a heavy sense of irony. When he visited George W. Bush shortly after his inauguration, he told him with some pride: "Well, I'm probably the first New Yorker to come and visit your White House, Mr. President." He visited several presidents there and told them that he prayed for them by name every day: "That sentiment was typical of Mychal," said Stephen Weaver. "He felt it reassured people who were feeling anxious or afraid, regardless of their status, that their concerns were held by him. I imagine it might have had some beneficial impact on the individuals concerned."

On Tuesday, September 28, 1999, Father Mychal was thrilled to be back in Washington for the annual breakfast with religious leaders. The hosts were President and Mrs. Clinton. He reported on the experience for the Holy Name Province newsletter and seemed to have absorbed every detail. In places his account was prophetic:

> I showed my invitation and my photo ID to the guard at 8 P.M. today (Sept. 28) and walked gingerly into the White House. I wanted to see everything. It was not important for me to mix with the other 129 "clergy leaders" from all over our nation. This was a special moment — I did not want to miss a trick.
>
> Leisurely, the President and Mrs. Clinton were moving among us. He held a coffee mug in his left hand, smiled, and looked deep into the eyes of all his guests as they greeted

him. As I have done on two other occasions, I promised him prayers each morning and night.

The crowd moved to Hillary, and he stood alone. Hugh, the young Irish immigrant from our kitchen, had asked me to get the President's autograph. This was the moment. I told him how to spell "Hugh," and he penned his name to my place card. I knew that Hughie would be thrilled.

As we entered the presidential dining room, I moved to my designated table only to find out that I was sitting next to Mrs. Clinton. The president sat at the table next to us, side-by-side with Archbishop Theodore McCarrick of Newark. The atmosphere was one of total relaxation.

The President gave us a gracious and warm welcome. Then he mentioned what he called "one of the most difficult years in my life." He told us of our importance as spiritual leaders. He admitted that he had been "profoundly moved, as few people have, by the pure power of grace, unmerited forgiveness through grace." He then spoke of the loving support of his wife, Hillary, and their daughter, Chelsea, and three of the clergymen who were present. "As all of you know, this has been a very difficult year for me and them, but by God's grace we are moving forward." The press departed — satisfied.

All in all, we had a delightful breakfast. What would they serve at the White House? This was the menu: "Fruit plate with peach sauce. Black walnut banana bread. Tomato, mushroom, and spinach omelet. Turkey sausage. Hash brown potatoes. Breakfast pastries. Coffee, tea, and juice."

Mrs. Clinton told me all about the new house in Chappaqua, the goodness of people helping to purchase it, and the challenge of the Secret Service to secure it. She moved on to speak of her visits to the Empire State and of the state's strengths and its problems.

I spoke of the City, the friars, the Fire Department, the Residences, and the Breadline. "I would love to visit the Breadline sometime," she said.

Later, I asked her for her menu, and she was happy to give it to me — first signing it. I was stunned when I saw she had my name written on it. How did she know who I was?

After we finished the breakfast, the President wanted the guests to respond to his remarks on the juvenile violence and the hate crimes in the nation so prevalent in these past years. The response was wonderful. Clinton then said, "We have time for one more response before I leave you to go to meet with the Turkish leader." Being so close to him, I raised my hand and he, smiling, pointed the microphone at me and said, "Father."

I first welcomed him, the First Lady, and Chelsea to the Empire State, as our new neighbors (applause). Then I thanked him for having me to breakfast in "our house" and how proud my immigrant parents would be to see me here today. This would be beyond their wildest dreams, as they came to know each other on the boat from Ireland.

"And I speak to all of the religious leaders today and urge us to recognize our need to be a part of all that has been said of the healing process, of the pain, of the hate crimes that have gripped the nation this past year. But please keep in mind that we are spiritual people and there is a tremendous need for us to be a 'people of prayer,' to be in constant contact with our God, whoever he or she may be. To teach our people more and more the values of personal prayer. So often, after the tragedy, we see pictures of our people, brokenhearted, holding hands in prayer. Why can't we have them do this *before* the tragedy — daily if possible."

I continued, "I would like to say just one word for the fellowship of Alcoholics Anonymous. It has done more good to heal more brokenness and tragedy and to avoid so much of the same in this country than all else. I said recently that Bill Wilson and Dr. Bob, its founders, have done as much good in this century or even more good than Mother Teresa — forgive the comparison. Why? Because A.A. is a spiritual program, not a religious program — religions often cause wars [applause] — and its members start to change their lives and grow spiritually and be in constant contact with their Higher Power. Prayer is so important to help the change to take place.

"I offer this for your consideration — we must be people of prayer before all else. And, Mr. President, that is our gift to you — our prayer for you and our nation."

"What you said is beautiful," replied the President, pointing the index finger of his right hand at me. "If I had the principles of Alcoholics Anonymous when I was a young boy growing up, I'm sure my family life, so scarred by the disease of alcoholism, would have been so different. Thank you!"

Stephen Weaver said Mychal admired Clinton because of his social policies. He was not able to have a very critical attitude toward the policies of Republican presidents because he was partly seduced by the glamour of office and of being able to visit the White House. He would always want to defend the fact that the president in his view personified all that was good about America and therefore was somehow beyond that sort of critique. He was a Franciscan who had made his own peace with the issue of how one could live the gospel in American society. It entailed giving his life to his ministry and embracing the promise of poverty that lay at the heart of the Franciscan charism. His version of political activism was working with the inner-city casualties of some of the injustices in American society and, through that solidarity, being able to share with people who were poor or cast out because of their status. He always shied away from overt political activity, not least because it was important for him to cultivate people of different political persuasions to promote the very work he was seeking to do in the name of the poor.

Father Anthony McNeill said that after Mychal Judge had led the prayer breakfast in the White House with the Clintons, he arrived in England with a bagful of gifts, including serviettes from the bathroom of the White House with their own gold presidential seal. He went to great lengths to describe the experience. He had stood up having prepared in his mind what he wanted to say, but when he had started to speak something different had come out. He spoke highly of the Clintons. He considered Bill Clinton a bright man, and he thought the pair were good people. "He wasn't really a politician," says Anthony McNeill. "Even when politics was going on in his community, he would rise above it. His phrase was: 'If you lie with dogs, you pick up fleas. Go with the winners. Leave the losers behind.'" But he ministered to the losers and helped to heal them.

WHEN ANTHONY MCNEILL was teaching at Campion Catholic High School at Hornchurch in Essex, he invited Mychal Judge to speak to the sixth form. He spoke to all the classes about the prayer breakfast with the Clintons and about his alcoholism:

> It was like watching a performer describing how God had moved in his life. It was a great testimony. The sixth formers were just awestruck at how free and open he was about his own personal and private struggles. He got down on his knees and said prayers to God for all the kids in the sixth form in front of them.

Mychal Judge also flew to Britain to attend Stephen Weaver's ordination to the priesthood. In the middle of a celebratory meal in the presbytery, a man of the road called at the door. It was clear he had been drinking and, in the course of the man's attempt to remonstrate with the person who opened the door, he fell over and struck his head. Mychal Judge, who had witnessed the scene, immediately went to support the man. Checking to see how he was, Father Judge picked him up, talked to him, befriended him, insisted on accompanying him to the emergency room of the local hospital, and then stayed with him until he had been seen. Stephen Weaver commented:

That really captures for me the way in which Mychal was able to suspend his tendency to self-dramatize so he could be fully present to the needs of people, in this case the poor. This was someone in whom he probably recognized his former self. In a very Christlike gesture, like the Good Samaritan, instead of passing him by, he chose to stay with him and tend his wounds until he was in his right mind again. One minute he had been playing court to an appreciative audience, the next reaching out with real compassion to someone who was suffering.

Friends, though, teased Mychal about always wanting to be in the limelight: he seemed drawn to cameras. Some accused him of not being the humble Franciscan he was supposed to be. He explained that he needed to connect with the media because that was the way he could spread the Word of Christ. "We always admired him for being that way, but he always had a bit of blarney in him," said Charles Galanaugh.

He always wore his Franciscan robe because he wanted to be recognized as a Franciscan. His relationship with religious authority was Jesus-like. He would be willing to confront the church's lack of attention to some of the problems Jesus would have been worried about — legalities and pomp and circumstance — but he did not think this was the real role of the church. He wanted to act out a life that was much more like the early Christ.

Certainly Mychal Judge appeared as an omnipresent Christian witness in the city of New York. The writer and raconteur Malachy McCourt said that wherever he went he would find Judge there too. He had tremendous resources politically, socially — and financially. According to McCourt:

He was very mischievous with money. He had a vow of poverty, so he would wonder, "How can I use this in the most efficient and efficacious manner?" He would get money from very conservative organizations that had the Irish habit of saying: "Here are a few dollars, Father. Use them as you see fit." Even these right-wingers liked him, but he would give their money to a gay organization as an anonymous contribution. And they wouldn't know.

While people did not regard him as an intellectual, this simple friar was well read and sharp, presenting himself as a left-wing liberal. He metabolized information well and could synthesize it. A fellow Franciscan who watched him operate on the margins came to regard him as "one of the smartest friars in New York and one of the most humble."

14

BROTHER FIRE

⟶ ⟞∞⟍ ⟝

DURING HIS LAST YEARS, St. Francis lived with the painful effect of the stigmata and agony in his lungs, stomach, and eyes. Nursed constantly by his close companions, he could neither rest nor sleep with ease. Intensifying his prayer, Francis gained reassurance that his suffering would be rewarded by a place in heaven. So he composed a song of thanksgiving, "The Canticle of Brother Sun," praising God for all creation:

Most high, almighty, good Lord,
Yours be the praise, the glory, the honor, and every blessing;
To you alone, most high, do they belong
And no man is worthy to utter your name.

Be praised, my Lord, with all your creatures,
Especially Lord Brother Sun,
To whom we owe both day and light,
For he is beautiful, radiant, and of great splendor;
Of you, most high, he is the emblem.

Be praised, my Lord, through Sister Moon and the stars,
You have made them in the heavens, bright, precious, and
     beautiful.

Be praised, my Lord, through Brothers Wind and Air,
Through cloud, clear skies, and all other weather
By which you give your creatures sustenance.

Be praised, my Lord, through Sister Water,
So very useful, humble, precious, and chaste.

Be praised, my Lord, through Brother Fire,
By whom you enlighten the night;
He is beautiful, merry, robust, and strong.

Be praised, my Lord, through our sister, Mother Earth,
Who sustains and looks after us,
Producing the different fruits, colored flowers, and the grass.

Father Mychal Judge was a fraternal presence to the New York
Fire Department for nearly a decade. He did not allow his own
struggles to keep him back from the front line. Appointed an
associate Catholic chaplain in 1992, he became chaplain two years
later. He brought the gentle spirit of St. Francis to the hard world
of fire fighting. "He was a living example of Francis. If there was
any type of argument or a little friction, his manner of speech and
action showed them there was a better way," said Father Bob Post,
chaplain to the Stamford Fire Rescue Department in Connecticut.

The job was a much-coveted position. Mychal Judge, who said
he would have become a fireman had he not become a priest, was
a natural candidate. After all, he had seemed to live with one ear
permanently cocked to the sound of a siren. With an instinctive
sense of the dramatic, he had the reporter's reactive streak. Father
Post explained:

> It's not that we chase fire engines. We follow firefighters into
> what they do. You have to have this feeling for adventure,
> although not like Pavlov's dogs — as if whenever we hear
> a siren, we respond. But there is something that attracts
> us. There is a little trigger that goes off, making us want to
> be part of this excitement and this scene. We never know
> when we turn that corner what we will see or find — or
> what will besiege us. Immediate decisions have to be made.
> Someone has been burned. A firefighter is being put into an
> ambulance. Anything can happen at any moment. We have
> to be aware of that beforehand.

The patron saint of firefighters and their chaplains, St. Florian, was a soldier in the Roman army at the time of the burning of Rome. He pulled many people from the fiery debris. In Italy, there is still a motto, *Ubi dolor, ibi vigiles:* Where there is sadness, there are firefighters. The aim of the Catholic fire chaplain is to provide spiritual assistance and pastoral guidance to members of the department in everyday situations as well as in personal difficulties and emergencies. They assist at weddings, baptisms, and funerals for the families of firefighters as well as caring for those who are injured or bereaved in fire tragedies.

Shortly after taking over as chaplain from the late Father Julian Deeken, Father Mychal was alerted during the night to police reports of a ship running aground and Chinese nationals with guns landing in the Rockaways. An honorary firefighter who accompanied him recalled:

> Just as we got to the Brooklyn-Battery Tunnel, the radio started to crackle with confirmation of a report of a large ship aground with passengers in the water. Mychal gunned the Chevy and hit the lights and sirens, both of which reverberated off the tunnel walls. I felt like I was in the middle of Studio 54. I said, "Mike, what are you doing? Slow down." He looked straight ahead and laughed: "No, this is good. I'm not sure what we've got here, but we can do good things together."
>
> I'll never forget what we saw that chilly morning. Helicopters in the air. A large broken ship battered by the waves offshore and a beach full of shaking, shivering, and soaked Chinese men. . . . They did not speak a word of English, and he did not speak Chinese, but it did not deter Mychal. Within a few minutes he was handing out blankets and coffee and telling jokes. And they laughed. An immigration officer warned him of the dangers of disease from the men — tuberculosis, hepatitis. Mychal said thank you, ignored the warning, and continued on as he was inclined to do.

Later, over a hearty breakfast, Father Mychal's companion commented: "Mychal. You're a bright guy. They could be very sick." The new chaplain replied: "When I travel halfway around the world, I get a blanket and cup of coffee. They're our guests and they deserve no less. They only want what we were born into."

Tom Ferriter recollected that Father Mychal had been working for only two weeks when he went out to a blaze and was not clear on his role. "He found some water, filled up a cup, and climbed a ladder to give a drink to a fireman with gallons pumping through his hose. They had to post a fireman at each ladder to keep him off it. He was unbelievable." Ferriter also recollected the day Father Mychal's appointment was endorsed at a high-profile event at Randalls Island at which a number of firefighters and officials were being promoted:

> I went and watched as all the people being promoted got rushed off the stage. Then the commissioner said: "Now for Mychal Judge." The place erupted. He was the star. That day he invited me to have a meal. "This is the one time in my life I can afford to buy lunch. You have to join me." There were eleven of us, power lawyers and politicians and me a poor businessman. We had lunch on the East Side, and he was so proud he could pay for it. He asked me to give the invocation. I said: "Here's to Mychal Judge's Brooklyn Irish mother, who got everything she wanted in life: a son with a Roman collar and a city job." He repeated that many times.

Fire chaplains were expected to establish and develop camaraderie, Father Post explained.

> Firefighters are different from police officers. They are a fraternity, almost like a religious community. They eat together and sleep in dormitories together. They are with each other for a whole shift. The fire chaplain, too, eats with them and at times stays overnight with them. He cheers on their sporting teams. He is one of them.

Mychal Judge used to say to Robert Post: "We just have to be ourselves as priests to the men." He felt chaplains should not put themselves on pedestals, but should nonetheless show they represent a special way of life. When Father Post visited fire stations in New York, he was struck by the number of times the men would eagerly ask: "Do you know Father Mike?" "He made an impression and had a tremendous influence. He related to them as guy-to-guy, man-to-man."

Although some firefighters could at times be sexist, racist, and homophobic, Father Mychal acted as a counterpoint to the machismo. Father Post explained:

> They are all into this macho thing. They're tough guys. But that's on the outside. If you cut to that core, you will find a beautiful heart willing to do anything. Mychal was the opposite of that real hard, tough, macho outside. But when his inside opened to their inside, it was the same beautiful heart. Franciscans have a special message and a way about them. They preach a message of love, not fear, of God. That was the message of his whole life.

To the men of Engine 1/Ladder 24, he was one of the family. He would come into the kitchen, eat dinner, and chat — joking all the time. But in times of emergency, the distinctive brown habit was replaced by black, fire-repellent attire and a sturdy white helmet. Firefighter Steve Wojciechowski knew Father Mike throughout his tenure.

> Every big job we had, you always turned around and there he was. He would speak to all the firefighters, but he would stay by all the chiefs so he got direct word if anything happened to any of the men. He wanted to be there and help out. All the chiefs knew him and loved him. He was just right in the thick of things. Sometimes people see a robe or a uniform and they will think certain things. But Father Mike was a human being. You could relate to him. I used to talk to him

about my family problems, and he used to give me advice. Other guys would talk about problems with their marriage or their kids. He was always a good listener and had a good memory. He would come to you later on and say: "How's that going in your life?" He once gave me advice with something and later told me: "Steve, you have done everything you could possibly do. You just have to leave it alone and leave it up to God now. If not it is going to destroy your life and you won't be able to function." So I took his advice and left it up to God.

He often talked to friends about the stress of having to arrive at a distant hospital in the dead of night to comfort the family of a firefighter burned or injured on the job. He referred to himself as a "Face": When dignitaries, such as the mayor, the fire commissioner, or a politician entered the hospital room as strangers and tried to console the family as well, Father Judge would ease their embarrassment. He would say: "I can see their eyes scan the room because they're uncomfortable. Then they come and stand beside me, because after all what can they do? The poor guy is lying there in awful shape and the wife is distraught. Just awful. So, I'm a face they can come to."

But Father Mychal was present at the funerals too. Steve Wojciechowski once drove him out to Long Island for the funeral of a firefighter who had died of a heart attack after shoveling snow. It was a long journey, so he arranged for him to stay overnight with his father in Smithtown. He met Steve's niece and nephew and blessed them.

That's how he was, a very gentle soul. These were the things he did behind the scenes of which people were not aware. I don't know how he did it all. He must have been overwhelmed at times, but he was very authentic, genuine, and sincere. After talking to him for five minutes, you would think you had known him ten years. He made everybody feel comfortable, warm, and welcome. He was the type of

guy you just let into your life. You opened the door, and
from there he just communicated with the firefighters all
around. With it came this sharp Irish wit. "You want to eat
with us?" we'd ask. "No," he'd joke. "I've gotta get home
for the mother-in-law. She's breaking my chops again. You
know how mothers-in-law are."

At funerals Father Mike seemed to have a presence that
"jumped out at you." Placing his spectacles on the top of the coffin, he would look toward the mourners and preach so intimately
they felt they were back in their living rooms. He brought out the
positive in a death or a tragedy and had a gift for cheering people
up in the worst of circumstances. He used it every day of his life.
He reached out and touched anybody he came into contact with.

Firefighter John Barnych, who works at the Lincoln Center
firehouse, has never forgotten the support Father Mike provided
after his thirty-seven-year-old brother, Harry, also a firefighter,
died of a brain tumor. He left a widow, Laura, and two children,
Lauren, eight, and Chris, six. On the day of the funeral, Father
Mike drove fifty-five miles north to Monroe in Orange County to
lead the service. John Barnych recalled:

> He related the death of his own father to the children. He
> made them smile and forget their troubles. I just saw the
> expression on their faces that lit up for a brief moment. That
> was a blessing in itself. He had words to console them. He
> had a real gift for getting through to people and making them
> feel comfortable. I never forgot that. It made a difference.

But one funeral was to prove a little more controversial. In
1994 Captain John Drennan of Ladder 5, at Houston and Sixth
Avenue, was seriously injured in a fire at a three-story residence.
He sustained burns to more than 65 percent of his body. Father
Mike would go to the burns unit and hold the captain's hand as
he lay in a state of heavy sedation. After being nursed for forty
days, Captain Drennan died at the age of forty-nine, leaving a

widow, Vina, and four children. Father Mike was a strong support to the family throughout the ordeal. "Mychal Judge felt there was something very special about the fortieth day," said Vina Drennan.

> There was always a presence of God in him, a peacefulness in the midst of fear, pain, and suffering. He had that gift of presence. Sometimes he would pray over John and felt God was listening. I used to feel the comfort of that wisdom. The love continued after John's death. He always knew when to call us — the anniversary of the death and even our wedding anniversary. I was really blessed to be his friend.

Father Mike said the Requiem Mass for John Drennan in St. Patrick's Cathedral. A friend who attended sensed the tension that day between him and Cardinal O'Connor:

> The cathedral is the cardinal's house, and he presides over it, but there was Father Mychal saying the funeral Mass. It was, as always, a wonderful, moving, spiritual, funny, and sad Mass. I don't think Cardinal O'Connor liked it very much because, at the end, he took the stage for a minute and asked John Drennan's son to turn around and watch as people applauded his father. But to me it seemed like the cardinal was saying: "This is my house and I have to get the additional attention." I think Father Mychal played into that as well. I think he always had a bit of competitive spirit. Cardinal O'Connor was not particularly fond of him. They just stayed away from each other. In any case, Mychal Judge did not answer to him but to the authorities of his own order.

THE RELATIONSHIP between Judge and O'Connor was never harmonious. Many feel the cardinal was envious of the Franciscan's popularity and irritated that he didn't minister by the book. He was sometimes called to account and was even groomed by a lawyer in the art of defense.

Individuals might approach him and ask if they should go to confession. He would say "No — general absolution" and then make the sign of the cross in front of them without requiring individual acts of repentance. On at least one occasion Father Mike had said Mass in the firehouse without wearing vestments. One of the firefighters, a traditional Roman Catholic, reported him to a priest friend. The complaint reached the ears of a young monsignor at the chancery. Soon afterward, a preliminary investigation was under way by the chancery. Mychal Judge received a letter asking: "Are you the Mychal Judge who does not wear vestments when saying Mass? Are you the Mychal Judge who gives general absolution? Are you the Mychal Judge...?" Infuriated, Judge soon repaid the pernickety bureaucrat. In a telephone call he said:

> This is Father Mychal Judge. I have been a priest for almost forty years now, and I am surprised to get this letter. If I have ever done anything to embarrass the church that I have served and loved so dearly all these years, if I have ever hurt or tainted her by what I have done, I would like to be burned at the stake on Fifth Avenue at the front doors of St. Patrick's.

A startled voice at the other end replied: "Well, now, calm down, Father Mike."

"No," Judge insisted. "I want to come and tell you this." The church official told him there was no need. Mychal Judge hung up and laughed hysterically. He figured he'd put the young clerical upstart in his place. Then, in characteristic form, he added: "It's sheer madness. Sheer madness."

Mychal Judge, who was a talented mimic, related the episode to full dramatic effect. One friar, Brian Carroll, said he considered the performance worthy of an Emmy:

> He got into trouble so often with the chancery because he made those who were cut from the red and scarlet cloth

feel uncomfortable. He had an ongoing feud with Cardinal O'Connor, who was intensely jealous of him because he would be asked to speak at funerals and events over the cardinal. No matter how many robes the cardinal put on or how much power he tried to exert, he still could not quiet or quash Mychal Judge because Mychal's simplicity spoke to people's hearts.

Nonetheless, Mychal Judge loved the Roman Catholic Church and had genuine respect for the pope, even though, according to friends, he disagreed with some of the teachings of the magisterium and could be critical of ecclesiastical power games. James Boyle, a former president of the Uniformed Firefighters Association, was intimately involved with Father Mike in breaking bad news and counseling families. He commented: "He had a style that infuriated the church leaders but one that was preaching Christ to help the less fortunate. The church was a hierarchical society and very rigid. Mychal was not rigid. That's what made him special and why everyone loved him. He was unique in every single way you could think of." Mr. Boyle lost his own firefighter son, Michael, on September 11, 2001. Mychal Judge had sent Michael notes of encouragement from the day he entered the fire service until a month before their deaths.

Being in the company of Mychal Judge was often a mood-changing and sometimes life-changing experience. Firefighter Tyrone Johnson singled out the "Father's Day" fire in Queens in which four firemen — all fathers — died. Father Mike was there for them, day or night:

> When he stepped on the scene, you felt a confidence in yourself because he always had a good word for everybody. If you were feeling down that day and he said a few words to you, you felt good. If you had a problem and talked to him, he reassured you that everything would be all right. If you were having a bad day, you looked forward to seeing him because he made your day much better.

But there was always a mischievous streak to "Brother Fire," whose New York tours in his fire department car rivaled anything the city tourist industry could have dreamed up. An Irish American friend, Michael Meenan, supposedly getting a ride to a gym, ended up on a high-speed tour of Chelsea. The car, with its head and rear lights flashing, tore through the neighborhood, zipping through traffic, and forcing cars to pull out of the way. "It reminded me of hitching rides on the back of buses in the Bronx or skipping wildly through the torrents of water pouring from a hydrant on a sweltering summer day. I knew Mychal felt the same Irish rebel glee as I did."

Several times Father Mike asked for radio checks from the central fire department dispatcher. Calling in on his official call sign, he received confirmation, mastering radio, lights, and the steering wheel all at the same time. "I loved him immeasurably when he was so carefree," said Michael Meenan. "But he kept admonishing me: 'Michael, you mustn't laugh. You mustn't. Someone will see you goofing around and write a letter in, saying some old white-haired guy was driving like a lunatic. I'll get into trouble. People will write down the license plate number.'"

But in real emergency situations, Mychal Judge ministered beyond the call of duty. One year he was guest of fire department chiefs who were holding a national convention in San Francisco, the West Coast city named after St. Francis. Emerging from his hotel one morning, he saw a man knocked down by a passing car and left battered and bleeding in the road. A number of people went to assist him, but it was Father Mike who went to pray by his side and spoke reassuringly to him until the ambulance arrived. He later checked out the man's location in the hospital and visited him there. He also made contact with the family, with whom he kept in touch for some time after the incident.

It was a perfect example of how Father Mike could not only keep a dramatic incident under control but transform it into a moment of grace.

15

SISTER DEATH

―⚬⚬⚬―

S T. FRANCIS regarded even death as a sibling. As he lay dying, he opened his arms and uttered: "She is welcome, sister death." Francis delighted in adding a final stanza to his "Canticle":

Be praised, my Lord, through our sister, the Death of the Body,
From whom no living man escapes.
Woe to them who die in mortal sin,
But blessed are they who do your holiest will,
For them the second death shall never harm.

Praise and bless our Lord, and give him thanks,
And serve him with great humility.

Five years before his own death and at a time when he was not in the best of health himself, Father Mychal Judge began an unexpected ministry to the bereaved. On Wednesday, July 17, 1996, a Paris-bound plane exploded shortly after takeoff from New York's JFK Airport and crashed over the waters off Long Island. All 230 passengers and crew on TWA Flight 800 perished. It was the nation's second worst air disaster. The sudden nature of the crash prompted speculation about a terrorist attack. Although this was later ruled out, sabotage appeared a distinct possibility at the time.

Father Mychal Judge was soon at a hotel near JFK Airport, among the clergy ministering to families and friends in shock and confusion. Up to a hundred people were gathered in a small ballroom. The mayor of New York, Rudolph Giuliani, went from table to table taking names and checking them against a list. "If the name wasn't there, people would have to sit and wait," Father

Mike recalled at the time. "I'd introduce myself, start a con-versation. They'd say a sentence, and then they'd start to cry. That went on until about 4:30 Thursday morning." He found his experiences of fire traumas helped him. While never completely comfortable, he was not ill at ease. "I'd walk over, sit down, and start to talk. And then let them talk. That's therapeutic."

The outbursts of pain, separation, anguish, fear, and love were wrenching. Father Mychal remembered that when one name was confirmed, a woman simply dropped her head onto the table and cried. He knelt down beside her. The grief seemed as deep as the waters where the wreckage floated.

Father Mychal's voice would break with emotion as he recounted speaking with people who could have come from anyone's family. "Finding I was a Franciscan, one guy said he had gone to our Bonaventure High School in Paterson. Then there was a young lady, just graduated from high school, whose family was going to Ireland by way of Paris. And an Asian girl, distraught over her boyfriend. They were going to get married." But "there was no rejection of God or anger at God." Cardinal O'Connor was also there. "He went from table to table, and was very gracious," said Father Mike in the same interview for Holy Name Province's *Special Report.*

Many on the flight had connected from other cities. Their rel-atives would not arrive until later. When Father Mychal returned to the hotel on the Friday, there were between 350 and 400 people waiting for news in a room that had no windows, fresh air, or tele-vision set. "I spoke with a fellow who was to take care of a couple's children while they flew to Paris and a family from Queens with a baby — everyone wanted to hold him because he was such a sign of life."

The depth of hurt and sorrow was expressed later when a safety report was made public. Father Mychal commented:

> It's about death, shock, and separation, not knowing if the bodies will be found, not knowing if they'll be able to see

them, to touch them, as one lady said. The medical exam-
iner's report was quite graphic. People cried out loud. I found
myself crying a number of times. I was feeling such pain with
them. They told me stories about their daughter or son or
husband or wife, and these people seemed so real to me that
I couldn't believe they were dead. Someone's talking about
a beautiful face that is now so broken, marred, and scarred.

At Mayor Giuliani's request, Father Mychal gathered rabbis,
priests, and ministers and, within twenty minutes, they had agreed
on an ecumenical prayer service for family and friends. It was held
on Sunday, July 21, at Hanger 208. Over two thousand people
attended, including the New York and New Jersey governors, and
Father Mychal presided. Prayers were in English, French, Italian,
Hebrew, and Spanish. He said it was important for the families
"to get closure for the week."

Mychal Judge returned to the hotel for fifteen nights, offering
his love and compassion to anyone who needed it. According to an
account in *Catholic New York*, one of the most difficult experiences
came a week after the crash when he was asked to say a prayer at
the same time as the explosion had happened — 8:47 P.M. "God
is present, loving, smiling, having received our loved ones," he
said in the hall of the hotel. "They are in his presence, illumined
by his smile, and warmed by his love. His kingdom is enriched
this day, so enriched by so many beautiful souls. So much beauty.
Our world is so empty without them. Our hearts are broken, our
sadness immense, our tears so abundant.... We live our sorrow
together."

Then he prayed to God: "We need You. Please come and touch
us. Fill us with courage, calm our discomfort, give us signs of Your
presence. We need to feel that You hear us as we offer You our
prayers and we try to overcome our grief.... We ask You, we beg
You, come."

He forged bonds with a number of families. When they asked
how God could have allowed the disaster to happen, he gently

reminded them that God desired only happiness. When something went wrong like this, there was another reason. He also marveled at people's faith, like a couple who lost their daughter and son-in-law and told Father Mychal that they would never be able to carry on without the Mass and the rosary.

Frank Carven lost his sister, Paula, and her son, Jay, who had been heading to Paris for the boy's ninth birthday. Paula, a flight attendant for TWA, was a devoted young mother. Jay had a voracious appetite for knowledge and was fascinated by the *Titanic*. Frank Carven, county attorney for Harford County, Maryland, recalled the chaos and confusion when his family arrived at the Ramada Inn the day after the crash.

> Hundreds of people were scrambling around the hotel, which was set up to be the emergency quarters. We were seated at a large round table and asked what religion we observed. My mother responded Catholic. Several minutes later, a large man with silver hair, sparkling eyes, and a gentle smile appeared. From that day forth he was our friend and confidant. He did not judge, preach, or pressure. He was there to listen, to console, to absorb the pain that we all felt. He was there for the families of that disaster from that terrible day to the end of his life.

Mychal Judge attended the funeral of Paula and Jay in Maryland and, a year after the crash, joined Paula's mother, Ann Carven, and other mourners who had traveled to Long Island for a seaside service of remembrance after a Memorial Mass in St. Patrick's Cathedral. He cried with them. A few months later, Father Mychal sent a thanksgiving card to Mrs. Carven. "Somehow," he underlined, "may it be a blessed, peaceful day. You have my love and prayers." In another letter he wrote: "Dear Ann, Peace and Good Health! Thank you for a blessed week — Heaven must have been quite some place these last few days — They will tell us about it some day. . . . Be at peace — The family is so blessed having you. We all are. Love, Mychal."

One year he sent Ann Carven an Easter Message, which he had written for friends. It provided a rare written insight into his thoughts on death and resurrection:

"Easter is wonderful. No hectic shopping for gifts. Just a few cards, no pressure... so different from Christmas." So said my sister Dympna to me on the phone last night. Smart woman. There is something important about our own personal preparation for the holy day.

Also *Lent*... the holy season of prayer and fasting. We are not always sure why we "give up" things... but we do. We want to be ready to give ourselves wholeheartedly for "the feast."

I think the powerful, mysterious fact of God loving us so much is exemplified in that he allows us humans (our forebears) to literally "beat him up" and kill him so that he can come forth from the dead, walk among us, and then ascend to open the gates of heaven for us. Only he could open them as God-Man, because they were shut closed from our side by our first parents. Jesus is our resurrection.

We have been given the right to the kingdom of heaven: is any one of us rushing into that kingdom? We are called to be free, to know that in our worst moments of human failure we are deeply loved by a forgiving God. I once told a friar that I could not understand how my two sisters love me so deeply. With all my faults, failings, and foibles, what could they see in me that makes them love me so generously and beautifully?

His response was so simple and clear. "Well, if you can't understand their earthly love for you, how can you expect to begin to know God's love for you?"

Beneath the message Father Mychal added a personal touch, expressing gratitude for a St. Patrick's Day card "with himself on the front." He went on: "The whole Irish mystique is such a puzzle but such a blessing. Your kind gift went to work immediately for a lad with AIDS — always something — Must be out of town Holy Week but in all of it I have you and the family in thought and prayer — I admire how you carry on." At Christmas 2000, he wrote a note on a card to Ann, praying "that 2001 will bring you a little special blessing of peace and that Paula and Jay will keep you close to them." The following February, in a letter to friends on the fortieth anniversary of his ordination to the priesthood, he ended with the words "I love you, bless you, and thank you." On Ann's, he underlined "love" and "bless" once, and "thank" three times "for the years of support, love, and prayers."

Reflecting on Father Mychal's ministry to the family, Ann Carven said: "He took us through a terrible time. We are so grateful." The last time Frank Carven saw Father Mychal was in July 2001, on Long Island, the fifth anniversary of the crash. He spent three days with the family. "He was the humblest man I have ever met," he says. "There was no pomp or circumstance with Father Mike. He was a forgiving man who lived by what he believed. His faith was unshakeable." In a letter to Frank Carven a month before his own death, Father Mychal wrote: "Life is a mystery — as we know so well — but it brings so many of us together. I am fortunate for all the Carvens. God Bless, Mychal."

The recollections of the Carven family serve only to testify to the priest's capacity, not only to care for others, but to continue to care. The Carvens would not have been the only family to be receiving his blessings, and yet they felt like they were the only people who mattered to him. Father Mychal stayed in touch with many of the families, writing Mother's Day cards to women who had lost their children and birthday cards to children still grieving their mothers.

He once said he could work twenty-four hours a day ministering to firefighters and their families. He suffered pangs of guilt if he could not accomplish all that he wanted. "It's endless. There is so much work to do," he once said. "They have very stressful jobs. As much as I can, I talk with them. That way I learn to hear them and listen to their anxieties and fears and how they deal or don't deal with those fears." Once he received a call informing him that a lieutenant had been killed by a falling tree on a highway in upstate New York. Accompanied by the man's fellow officers, he went to break the news to his wife. She sat in a chair, and he knelt next to her. She asked him if he might have been killed by a tree because she had passed an accident that afternoon but hadn't stopped to look. "What could I say? It was very hard that time and it's hard each time."

ALTHOUGH HE KEPT a spiritual journal and scribbled countless notes to people, Father Mike was never a disciplined writer. He liked typing even less. There are therefore few personalized accounts of his ministry. However, in the *Firefighters' Newsletter*, 2001, an article, "In the Blink of an Eye," gave a rare glimpse into Father Mike's world, focusing not on him, but on those he was supporting:

> It was late Saturday evening, December 15th of last year when the Notification Desk called to say that a Battalion Chief was in a terrible accident in upstate Florida, New York. "A Chief, Keith Mallon, was thrown from his car, is badly injured, and is now being flown to Westchester Medical" was the message I received.
>
> When I arrived at the hospital, I saw Battalion Chief Richard Goldstein, who introduced me to Laura, Chief Mallon's wife. Laura is a real Fire Department wife: open, energetic, and to the point. She was trying to console Scott, one of her sons, and Corrie, a daughter, who the Chief was on his way to pick up from her soccer game, when the icy road caused the terrible accident. Laura was later to tell me, "I knew it was serious, when I saw they sent in you, the Big Guy."
>
> After a long wait, they let us in to see the Chief. Incredible! He was in such very good spirits — I have never seen him in any other way. Looking back on it, when we saw

him, we were gazing on a man who would not ever — or at least for now — do something he had done so naturally a few hours earlier, walk as he willed.

The Chief and Laura and the kids, too, could never have imagined that night how radically different their family and personal lives would be in the months ahead.

But they are such strong, very strong people, with deep faith. I admire them so much. They keep moving on. They still reach out to help others. Their sons and their daughters (Kevin, Jr., is a lawyer in California, Scott is a union apprentice electrician, Jill is a student at SUNY New Paltz, and Corrie — so sweet — a student in Warwick High School) are their main concern. The welfare of "those on the job" and their neighbors is so very important to them, and all these months later, with their faith and determination, "their lives are good," as the Chief told me this morning.

Chief Mallon, like all of us, loves "the job" so much and misses being away for now. I have come to admire and respect him so much — he whose life so radically changed in the blink of an eye, but who keeps them open to the new good life ahead.

When Father Mike's natural commitment to others is considered, it is astonishing to think that anyone should have wanted to block his appointment as fire chaplain unless they were envious of him. But, curiously, there had been some initial resistance. Stories about his ministry to the sick and injured, dying and bereaved would fill volumes. He encountered chaos and stilled the storm: "I walk right in, hold a hand, wipe a tear, and say a prayer. That's not me, Mychal Judge. That's the grace of God. I don't worry about the details or arrangements. It's a mystery. It's God."

Whoever came into contact with Father Mike in the shadow of Sister Death never forgot him. Even more remarkable was the fact that he never forgot them.

16

"BLESSED ARE
THE PEACEMAKERS"

———⬥———

M YCHAL JUDGE was made for New York, and New York was
made for him. But he also liked his Irish identity and imper-
sonated the accent in the yarns he could spin. Irish friend Brendan
Fay said Judge was always slipping into catchphrases such as
"How's himself?" and " 'Tis himself." He loved his Irish heritage
and took great pride in it, said Fay:

> You would often see him at various events with the Irish
> community and celebrations of Irish heritage. He would
> exclaim: "What a great heritage. Great people." Everything
> was "great" with Mychal. He would speak about the faith, the
> struggle, the history of Irish people, Irish immigration, and
> the struggle of Irish people to find their place in American
> culture.

Although famed for his work among firefighters, it was a long
Irish American friendship with a New York City police officer that
galvanized another public mission. In July 1986 Steven McDonald
had been on routine plainclothes patrol in Central Park when he
noticed three teenagers acting suspiciously. He approached one of
the youths, who pulled a .22 snubnosed pistol and shot him three
times. The young cop, married with his first child on the way,
was so severely wounded that he was not expected to survive.
His fight for life became national news. But after months in the
hospital and rehabilitation, he survived as a quadriplegic with no
sensation below the neck. He needs a tracheostomy to breathe.

Father Mychal came into Steven McDonald's life shortly after the shooting. He had just returned from his year in England and volunteered to take his turn in a rotation of priests who would visit McDonald in his room at Bellevue Hospital and say Mass. McDonald, a devout Catholic, couldn't speak at the time. After McDonald was transferred to Craig Hospital in Englewood, Colorado, for specialist care and treatment, Father Mychal paid him a surprise visit on his way back to New York from California. That afternoon McDonald was having a picnic with the International Police Association at the Cherry Creek Reservoir but Father Mychal found his way out to the woods. McDonald, who was speaking again by then, was so shocked to see him he couldn't remember his name. "Father, what are you doing here?" he asked. Father Mike was also surprised: "Oh, Steven," he said. "I've never heard you speak. You have a beautiful voice." A few months later Father Mike flew back to Craig to celebrate Mass for Steven and Patti Ann McDonald's second wedding anniversary and hear them renew their wedding vows.

In the years that followed, Father Mike was a regular visitor to the McDonalds' home on Long Island and became particularly close to their son, Conor, with whom he exchanged correspondence. Through careful spiritual guidance he also helped McDonald forgive the youth who had shot him. In 1988 Father Mychal accompanied Patti Ann on a European pilgrimage to the Marian holy places of Fatima in Portugal, Lourdes in southwestern France, and Medjugorje in Yugoslavia. They also visited Rome and took part in a papal audience. He asked John Paul II to touch Steven McDonald's wedding ring, which the pontiff then blessed.

But it was the missions Father Mychal undertook with Steven McDonald to Northern Ireland a decade later that were to seal his reputation as a spiritual envoy for peace and reconciliation. Intensely proud of his heritage, he was sensitive to the plight of people who lived in the North. Abhorring violence of any kind, he supported the Good Friday Agreement and hoped to see a united Ireland.

McDonald had long wanted to travel there to speak on forgiveness and nonviolent conflict resolution. He invited Johann Christoph Arnold, pastor of the Bruderhof, and other members of that Christian community to join him. Over three consecutive summers, they made three visits talking to groups, churches, and politicians, including the Irish prime minister Bertie Ahern; Gerry Adams and Martin McGuinness of Sinn Fein; and Dr. Ian Paisley, leader of the Democratic Unionist Party. They also met Nobel Peace Prize–winner Mairead Corrigan Maguire.

Project Reconciliation was undertaken in 1998 and 1999, followed by Journey to Forgiveness in 2000. The first trip happened just days after a terrorist bomb had exploded in Omagh. Father Mychal led a group in prayer and walked down one of the streets with a local parish priest. The families and friends of the victims seemed instantly attracted to the friar who had equal time for Protestants and Catholics. In Belfast they walked through a city park. McDonald remembered Father Mike reaching into his pocket and giving money to the homeless. He also bought them food from a vendor.

When they returned to Northern Ireland in 2000, they were joined by the choir "Kids for Peace." It was apparent that Mychal Judge hoped and believed that common ground could be established and that the many sides could come together building on what they shared. His choice of reading the psalms, which he did at all meetings, demonstrated this. He seemed to have a natural acceptance for anyone who came along, whatever their denomination or description. He easily met them where they were. "It was obvious his faith was not a pie-in-the-sky program," observed Arnold. "He showed his beliefs by reaching out to the person next to him. He demonstrated how he could meet anyone on their own ground and make them feel completely at ease. He was a real role model for young people today."

At every gathering, Father Mychal would recite a prayer attributed to St. Francis:

Lord, make me an instrument of thy peace!
Where there is hatred, let me sow love;
Where there is injury, pardon;
Where there is doubt, faith;
Where there is despair, hope;
Where there is darkness, light;
And where there is sadness, joy.

O divine Master —
Grant that I may not so much seek
To be consoled, as to console;
To be understood, as to understand;
To be loved, as to love.
For it is in giving that we receive,
In pardoning that we are pardoned,
And in dying that we are born to eternal life.

This was the spirit in which the fifty-strong peacemaking force arrived in the village of Drumcree, near Portadown in County Armagh, in July 2000 at the height of the marching season. Tensions were again running high. The July anniversary parade to Drumcree Parish Church is the oldest of its kind in the world. The first parade there by the Orangemen of Portadown District took place in 1807.

The Orange Order is the largest Protestant organization in Northern Ireland and believes marching is an essential part of its culture. It was founded in 1795 after a Protestant victory at Loughgall, County Armagh, in what became known as the Battle of the Diamond. The Order's name was chosen to commemorate the victory of the Protestant King William of Orange over the Catholic King James in the Battle of the Boyne on July 12, 1690. The Orangemen, in their bowler hats and orange sashes, claim they have a right to march down the Garvaghy Road in their traditional route back into the center of Portadown after their annual church service at Drumcree. The Catholic Garvaghy Road Residents' Coalition think the parade should be rerouted. The area has been subject to demographic change with Protestants moving out and Catholics moving in. In recent years the march has caused tension and violence. An essentially local issue has had much wider political ramifications.

After being searched by British soldiers, the peacemakers from America were given permission to walk up the Garvaghy Road to Drumcree Church, where they met the Church of Ireland rector, the Reverend John Pickering. Steven McDonald told *Irish Voice* that outside Drumcree Church they encountered Loyalist protestors with weapons. "I was physically shielded from them so they started to shout at Father Mike. 'We don't allow people like you in here,' they screamed. They were threatening him, and here he was in his priest clothing. But Father Mike just looked at them and smiled. And then he went into the church as planned."

The choir assembled at the front of the church and sang. There were prayers and Bible readings, one of them given by Mychal Judge. "He was a very striking character and stood out from the rest," John Pickering told me:

> He was a quiet and serene man. He appeared to me to be very understanding. He seemed to me to be very much observing and listening. They could not stay for long, but it was not rushed. The primary reason they came was to pray and let it be known that they would be continuing in prayer. They could have stayed at home in the States but the fact that they chose to come to Northern Ireland had much more effect. They wanted to be a great support to us. We always regarded it as a great privilege that they came.

Johann Christoph Arnold remembered the occasion for its "wonderful ecumenical prayer meeting between Catholics and Protestants that to my understanding hadn't happened for hundreds of years." Wherever there was a conflict between two sides, he pointed out, a peace mission had to go and understand the need, pain, and suffering that each endured. This was often extremely difficult, requiring sensitivity and skills of

listening. "One of Jesus' greatest commandments is 'Blessed are
the peacemakers.' One thing that Father Mike, Steven, and I often
discussed was that if we make only one peacemaker and bring a
little bit of peace where there has been a conflict, then our trip
will have been worth it." They also talked about how true peacemaking necessarily involved an active proclamation of forgiveness
and love as the only corrective to violence and hatred. Forgiveness was a power and not a weakness — the best preparation for
death and eternal life.

Arnold said Father Mychal showed no fear of death, especially
the day they walked up Garvaghy Road:

> The blue jackets of U.N. observers were all around and there
> was real tension about the presence of an R.U.C. [Royal
> Ulster Constabulary] member. Still Father Mike was relaxed
> and would not have thought about anything other than sup-
> porting his wheel-chair-bound friend. For the first time a
> group walked the length of the Garvaghy Road, meeting
> for prayer with the Catholics at one end, and again at the
> other end with Protestants and Orangemen. For Father Mike
> that was a very positive step forward. He entered into the
> experience with a sense of peace and certainty.

In a speech he gave during that visit to Northern Ireland,
Father Mychal revealed his ecumenical vision. He said that when
people got to heaven, God would not ask which denomination
they had subscribed to but only how much they loved him and how
much they had shared their life with others. He could not imagine
a God of love and reconciliation questioning people about their
religious allegiances. But in the human condition such divisions
persisted for reasons of power and control:

> People want to rule over other people and have God on
> their side, and if you are not on their side, then God's not
> on your side and all these sides. When you think about it, it
> is a tremendous waste of time and energy and all it does is

cause wars and then people get killed and families get divided and everything goes wrong. That's kind of how I look at this country and at home. And I know it's real and I know it's here and it's centuries old and it's very, very complicated. As simple as I see it, it's very complicated. So Steven asked me to come along, and Father Peter and Mary and Pat the nurse, Dennis, we've all come to show you we are praying for you. You have no idea of the thousands of prayers that every Saturday evening and Sunday morning and Sunday evening that go up to God from the churches of North America, for peace and unity in Northern Ireland. You hear it over and over again: "For peace and unity in Northern Ireland, let us pray to the Lord; let us pray to the Lord, for peace and unity in Northern Ireland." This little territory is known the world over. So with all those prayers and a loving, kind God who wants us to be at peace with each other, there has to be a solution coming. There will always be the people who want to destroy what God builds up through good people, but God will overcome. And God someday — I don't know how he is going to do it — but he's going to make the headlines rather than the devil. He will in the end, so don't give up. We pray together, we hold hands together, we believe together, we love together, we're saved together, and God reigns. Amen.

The Bruderhof, an international Christian community founded in Germany in 1920 by Arnold's grandparents, grew out of the Anabaptist tradition, which separated itself from the Roman Catholic Church in the sixteenth century. There has been little communication over the years. As a farewell for one of the peace missions, Father Mychal presided at a Catholic Mass in the grounds of the Bruderhof community at Rifton, New York. "This was a historic first," Arnold recalled. "Many of the Catholic faithful in our area came, and we celebrated the Mass together with Catholics and Anabaptists alike. We experienced a real feast of the Holy Spirit."

After their final trip in 2000, Father Mychal asked Steven McDonald for help in fulfilling a long-term dream — Irish citizenship. Although Irish law already considered him a citizen by virtue of his parents' birth in County Leitrim, he would not be completely at peace until he completed the formal procedures. McDonald said the day Mychal Judge finally received his Irish passport in the mail was one of the proudest in his life.

Mychal Judge and Steven McDonald had hoped to take their words of peace to Israel. Father Mychal had been to the Middle East in July 1993 as part of a thirty-strong interfaith delegation with the then mayor of New York, David Dinkins. New York attorney Brian O'Dwyer brought to mind the occasion when they accompanied Father Mychal to the Church of the Nativity in Bethlehem, the birthplace of Jesus:

> He made us all stand around holding hands and singing "Silent Night." That evening he took us to the Western Wall, the most sacred place of Judaism, and we all prayed together to our one God there. After that a tremendous bond came between us. He affected my life greatly, and he affected the lives of the people who were there. He took what had started out as essentially a political trip and turned it into an intensely spiritual experience — all by himself.

During the visit, Father Patrick Fitzgerald was admitted to the Hadassah Hospital cardiac unit with a suspected heart attack. He stayed for a week and spent a further two weeks convalescing in the King Solomon Hospital before being advised to return home. "Father Mychal stayed with me for my entire stay in Jerusalem," he recalled. "I took it easy while Mychal visited the holy places every day and visited the friars at Holy Sepulchre Monastery. After I returned home to New York, an angiogram showed no signs of a heart attack or muscle damage."

THE SERENITY of Mychal Judge brought peace to friends and strangers, at home and abroad. He was a wounded healer who

could relate to all people, not just his own circle. He tried to rec-
oncile where there was dissonance and offer peace where there
was strife. But it was a ministry that flowered from poverty, not
riches, from weakness, not strength. Wherever he was in the
world, Mychal Judge shared the spirit of St. Francis, of whom
it was said that he looked for the poor in everybody. William
Hart McNichols explained that once Mychal Judge discovered
how poor a person was he could relate to that person: "He could
go to a really wealthy person and see that they were poor in spirit,
lonely, or did not have a relationship with God. Then he could
look at the poorest person and see they had the greatest riches
precisely because they had the wealth of knowing God."

Father McNichols said that the world had given Mychal Judge
his wounds, but God had transformed them through his ministry
of peace and healing for others.

IV

Part Four

SERAPHIC LOVE

...As soon as that hand, which had been pierced and en-
kindled by the Seraph, touched the man, all sense of cold
left him.

— *The Fourth Consideration on the Holy Stigmata*

17

ANAM CARA

⎯⎯⎯∞∞⎯⎯⎯

May you be blessed with good friends.
May you learn to be a good friend to your self.
May you be able to journey to that place in your soul where
    there is great love, warmth, feeling, and forgiveness.
May this change you.
May it transfigure that which is negative, distant, or cold in
    you.
May you be brought in to the real passion, kinship, and
    affinity of belonging.
May you treasure your friends.
May you be good to them and may you be there for them;
    may they bring you all the blessings, challenges, truth,
    and light that you need for your journey.
May you never be isolated; but may you always be in the
    gentle nest of belonging with your *anam cara*.

THIS IS A FRIENDSHIP BLESSING from *Anam Cara*, a book of
Celtic wisdom by the Irish writer John O'Donohue. *Anam* is
the Gaelic word for "soul" and *cara* is the word for "friend." In the
Celtic world, *anam cara* was the soul friend, a person who acted
as a teacher, confessor, companion, or spiritual guide — someone with whom you could share your innermost self. According
to O'Donohue, there is a great need for a soul friend in everyone's life: "In this love, you are understood as you are without
mask or pretension. The superficial and functional lies and half-
truths of acquaintance fall away. You can be as you really are."
The Celtic tradition recognized that through such friendships,
graced with affection, the heart learned "a new art of feeling."

When two people came together, an ancient circle closed between them. They came, not with empty hands, but with hands full of gifts for each other. Often these were wounded gifts, awakening the dimension of healing within love. According to O'Donohue: "When you really love someone, you shine the light of your soul on him or her. We know from nature that sunlight brings everything to growth. If you look at flowers early on a spring morning, they are all closed. When the light of the sun catches them, they trustingly open out and give themselves to the new light."

A friendship with Mychal Judge was always a transforming experience. He was the *anam cara* for the postmodern age, a guide of souls and someone with whom you could dare to be yourself. Within the friary on Thirty-first Street, he and his Franciscan brother Father Patrick Fitzgerald were confessors to each other, celebrating the sacrament of reconciliation in their rooms for fifteen years:

> It just happened spontaneously and without appointment. We developed a pattern according to the liturgical year — Advent, Christmas, Lent, Easter, Pentecost. We would decide who was going first and then pray the penance together. It also happened on our birthdays, the anniversary of our ordinations, the feast of the Blessed Mother on August 15, the feast of St. Francis on October 4, or on the anniversary of Mychal beginning the road to sobriety. Our friendship was celebrated in a sacramental way as persons called to faith, called to priesthood, and gifted with friendship. We also went out to dinner with one another and would take long walks in the evening. Deep within the friendship there was a sacred sharing and a trust.

Another Franciscan, Father Anthony McNeill, whose home is in Britain, classed Mychal Judge as his own *anam cara* — "that person who stands alongside you as you go through life and shares experience." When Father McNeill made his solemn vows in 1986, he and his sister, Patricia, traveled to France with Mychal

Judge. He remembered Father Mychal getting irritable because he hadn't eaten.

He had that hungry, angry, and tired look. We stopped in a medieval town, bought French sticks with cheese, and sat on our coats at the side of the road. We had a simple meal. We were happy to sit, eat, and philosophize about life. Then we went to Paris, went into Sacre Coeur and lit candles. Mychal made his prayers vocally for people and mentioned them by name, especially Steven and Patti Ann McDonald. We stayed in the cheapest hotel he could find. He carried very little. His friend, Peter Daly, who had been a singer and actor, got us into the Lido to see the Bluebell Girls.

For Anthony McNeill, Mychal Judge was a father figure who showed him much affection and strengthened his self-confidence. What Father Mychal lacked in his own life, he became for other people. He could see people's good qualities, their talents, and their gifts. If people were not aware of those characteristics in themselves, Mychal was compelled to enable people to see the good within. "He knew what was happening within people. He would listen a lot as well. He always had things going on in his mind. He had things he wanted to do and he was ticking things off in his mind as he was doing them."

When Father Anthony was ordained a priest in 1987, Father Mychal traveled to Glasgow in Scotland for the first Mass and continued to support him in his ministry. When Father Anthony was later struggling as a parish priest in a poor area of Scotland's capital, Edinburgh, Father Mychal would phone him from America to support him. "Just to hear him say, 'I will pray for you this evening and mention you by name every evening,' somehow gave me strength — to know he was there." Mychal Judge was sincere. He would tell a friend the truth. "To get the affirmation of someone who had been through so much in his own life meant a lot because he was real," said Father McNeill. "He wasn't pretentious. He knew what it meant to struggle, to be down and out, to pull himself together when he had suffered and nobody had cared. He had done it himself with God's grace and his friends."

For all the bleaker times, Father Mychal never lost his sense of wonder. Father Anthony remembered one Christmas outside Rockefeller Center in New York, when Father Mychal told him to close his eyes, turn around, open them again, and look in awe at an incredible building with a Christmas tree on it. "He took great pleasure in watching people enjoying the wonder and beauty of life. He always had great excitement about going someplace new or doing something different. He had a great energy for a man of his age. A man of sixty-two, he was like someone who was twenty. I could not keep up with him in New York. His feet didn't stop, and I was exhausted."

It was Anthony McNeill who encouraged a talented British singer and actor, Roger Wright, to look up Mychal Judge while he was working as a model in New York. Before long the friar had taken him under his wing and a new spiritual friendship was forming. "It took me a few times to catch him," recalled Roger Wright, "but when I did he said: 'Oh, Roger: I've been expecting your call. Well, listen, you've gotta come up to the friary and come to Mass. Then let's go and have lunch.'" In between castings, Roger managed to connect with Mychal Judge, who promptly presented him with *Miracles Do Happen,* a book by Sister Briege McKenna:

> He was a very warm character, a fatherly figure who made sure I did not feel alienated in the bright lights of New York. At a time when I was alone, he comforted me. I will keep in my heart the warmth of this beautiful person. For me that was spiritual enlightenment in itself. He was the epitome of a person who welcomes strangers, just as Jesus would have done. I was a stranger, and he just opened his arms and welcomed me.
>
> He made me feel very comfortable, as though I had known him forever. He had a wonderful sense of humor. He took me out for a spin in his fire car and showed me Brooklyn

Bridge. He had just had a major heart operation and said how lucky he was to be alive. He was on a new spiritual journey. He told me how proud he was that he had met the Clintons, but he was humble about the people he knew. You could see, just looking into his eyes, that he had a real deep love for God. The first thing we did was pray together. He asked God to bless me and take care of me.

The last time Roger Wright met up with him, Father Mychal presented Roger with another sweater and a guitar. But it was many years before Roger came to read the book on miracles he had originally received, although he had kept it in a special place on his shelf. In the summer of 1999, Roger broke his toe on the London stage of *The Lion King* and suddenly remembered the title of the book. "I realized this was the time, and I read it in a day," Roger told me in London's Covent Garden before an evening performance. "The words were so powerful. They were about trusting in God, to believe he has a plan for you and that, through sickness, whether in body, mind, or spirit you receive healing. Little did I realize that what he gave me then would be such a great help to me when I broke my toe."

FATHER MYCHAL became spiritual director to Brother Thomas, S.S.F., after he had applied to join the Anglican Franciscans. They saw each other once a month for forty-five-minute sessions. Brother Thomas found him a great listener, calm and contemplative. He often observed his offhand delivery: "You know, Tom, let's sit down and spend a little time with the Lord."

A novice to the world of religious community, Brother Thomas learned much from Father Mychal about living with a group of men under vows. He approached the subject with humor and depth:

He knew that I was trying to have an encounter with God through the men I was living with, but people bring their illnesses and dysfunctions with them into community. He never explicitly told me that he loved living in community per se. I know he had some really close friendships among his brothers. He stressed it was important to find a soul mate with whom you could unload and talk. He took a lot of nourishment from that.

Father Mychal was the first person to teach Brother Thomas how to walk down a city street in a medieval habit. He told him it was important to look people in the eye and say "Hi!" As a walking icon of Franciscanism, he would deliberately acknowledge a person who stared at him. He had to make a connection before he could move on.

Mychal McNicholas, who changed the spelling of his name from "Michael" to "Mychal" after Father Judge's death, felt a bond with him because he too was a recovering alcoholic. Although he had been in sobriety for many years, McNicholas had abandoned his Catholic faith. Troubled, he went to see Father Mychal: "I went into this room with him and told him my story. I really went there to get absolution. I wanted to return to the church. After he gave me absolution and blessed me, I was an entirely different person. I thanked him for absolution. He said, 'I didn't give you absolution. You were ready yourself for it. You gave it to yourself. I was just here to bless you.'"

In 1999 McNicholas was diagnosed with cancer and understandably frightened. His doctor said he would try to save his life, but he still sought the consolation of Father Mychal. On a beautiful spring afternoon in New York's Central Park, McNicholas recounted the priest's words to him that day:

> He told me not to worry about it. God was going to take care of me. Once when I was in the hospital, he came to visit me wearing his fire gear and blessed me. I was in so much pain but so grateful and honored that my friend was there. I just knew he was somebody special. He was really Christ's representative on earth. You knew there was something different about him from other priests. We always hugged. Hugs keep

us drunks sober. When he put his arm around you and gave you a hug, you knew you were safe. All that fear just disappeared. He would say: "Don't worry. Don't worry. One day at a time. God will take care of you. His blessed mother will take care of you too. If you ever need anything, just call on God or his holy mother, Mary, and they'll take care of you."

Father Mychal helped rekindle McNicholas's commitment to the Catholic Church. He told him there was "a new church coming," but McNicholas sensed that any person who met the Franciscan or his fellow friars would know what that new church was:

There was hope. All we in sobriety look for is hope. The new church was one that was open. If you committed adultery, robbed a bank, or cursed your mother, you weren't going to go to hell. You would be forgiven. God would take care of those fears and put them away. All you would have to do was ask.

THE AUTHOR Malachy McCourt also found his religious convictions bolstered by his friendship with Mychal Judge. He came from atheism to a belief in a higher power through A.A., and Mychal Judge was influential in that.

Whatever God we chose, he was happy with that. So long as we had a spiritual life, that was fine with him. My faith in the God I have has been strengthened through my friendship with him. He would say, "That's good, Malachy. You're doing well there, kid." My God is some power greater than myself who doesn't judge me, doesn't test me, does not taunt me, does not tease me, knows what I am, knows where I came from, knows where I am going, and says, "You're okay, kid."

Once when McCourt had become severely depressed, he discovered more than a sympathetic ear in Judge, who commented: "I know all about that. I have been through that." He told McCourt that, if he "remained sober and kept doing what you're doing," he would guarantee he would come out of the trough and be all the better for it. He would look back on the abyss with a degree of satisfaction that he had managed to come through it and would be able to use the experience as a means of going forward. "Hope was always there. It was very comforting."

McCourt pointed out that there was never anything remotely malicious or vicious about Mychal Judge:

> If you were having a chat with him, he always made you feel as though you were teaching him something. His own presence was so gentle that you felt a peace in his company. That is what I always got from him. He wasn't one to go around giving advice. He wasn't that kind of a man at all. He had experienced much turbulence in his life but had come to terms with it. There was a serenity about him that was pervasive. In his company you would feel like breathing.

After almost every meeting, friends would be sent notes, which were hard to read because of Judge's almost indecipherable handwriting: "I was struck by what you said the other night and I wanted to tell you I much appreciated you sharing that." McCourt observed: "Everybody seemed to get these notes. He used to send out hundreds of them. It must have cost him a fortune in stamps unless he cajoled the post office into mailing them for him, which wouldn't at all have surprised me."

18

THE COURAGE TO BE

———— ∞∞∞ ————

G ROWING UP in an Irish Catholic working-class neighborhood in the Bronx barely prepared Michael Meenan for life
as a sober gay man. Talk of sexuality in any guise was taboo.
That he might one day fall in love with another young man was
unimaginable.

Meenan explained that his sexuality developed in "a bottom-
less chasm where the refreshing light of the sun never shone," a
state of nothingness he likes to refer to as a "cognitive void." He
had begun drinking heavily as a twelve-year-old, scraping money
together with his grammar school buddies to make illicit pur-
chases of beer or cheap vodka. They got their marijuana from
drug dealers in rundown tenements who slipped nickel bags of
weed through the peephole of dented front doors after they'd
received their price.

"I am unable to extricate my journey as a gay man from my
journey as an alcoholic," said Michael. "It would be like asking me
to renounce my ethnicity or the color of my eyes, or rendering an
accurate account of American history without mentioning slavery,
the Constitution, or World War II."

During the course of his recovery from alcoholism, Michael
Meenan, who was twenty-six, met Father Mychal Judge, fifty-
nine. From Judge's looks and accent, Meenan could tell he was an
Irish American New Yorker. Only much later did he discover he
was a Catholic priest. During Michael's initial months of sobriety,
Mychal Judge's "double-digit" sober time and gregarious personality irritated him. He understood he needed to attend meetings
to abstain from alcohol, but he wasn't particularly interested in

making chums in the process. Nonetheless, Mychal Judge soon became an invaluable member of an inner circle with whom Michael was able to share "the joys, challenges, and mystery" of being a sober gay man in the tumultuous world of New York City. "That Mychal was gay, sober, Irish American, and utterly outspoken about his experience, strength, and hope as a priest and as a gay man became an absolute gift in my life," said Michael:

> It was an unasked-for blessing that God allowed me to share. Meeting him was a godsend because he was living proof that I was not a freak of nature. To find another Irish American gay man, who shared so many of the same values I held, including a fierce endearing pride in our ethnicity, was very liberating. He made me realize that a life of serenity, joy, and communion with God and other people was indeed not only possible, but inevitable were I to remain sober and honest. And he gave me the courage to embrace my sexuality as one of God's most precious gifts.

Over the years Mychal Judge, like so many Irish men, defused any tension in the friendship through his contagious sense of humor. Laughter was the wounded healer's balm. He teased Michael Meenan constantly about the young man's own sense of self-importance, his insecurity with his looks, his sudden bursts of anger, self-pity, and doubts, and his seeming omniscience, which the friar's hard-won wisdom exposed. Almost every conversation ended with reassurance from Father Mychal: "Michael, if nobody told you today that they love you, let me tell you: I love you and God bless." It took Michael Meenan years of being comfortable with his own masculinity and sobriety before he was able to mutter the same words back to the priest:

> There were plenty of times when I felt like I had done egregious things that I was ashamed to admit to myself, never mind discuss with a man I honored as a Catholic priest. On several occasions, my conversations with Mychal included

my struggles with the men with whom I had had relationships. Mychal's advice always centered on his core belief that I needed to bring God more intimately into my life. I had to include God in a "working" fashion in my relationships, not to hoard my love and tenderness, but to share it with another and do so gloriously.

Michael Meenan was never one to list his sins behind a curtain but pointed out that, if he ever had a confessor, Mychal Judge was the man. There were occasions when he needed to unburden himself of guilt over matters that had plagued his conscience for years. But never did he feel judged.

My conversations with him only increased my recognition of God's indelible presence in my life — in the people he brought me into contact with, the situations I endured in order to mature and recommit myself to my values, and in the embrace of my homosexuality, which has informed me of my humanity and spiritual connection to God.

The Franciscan did not flaunt his sexuality, nor did he hide it or apologize for it. He integrated it into his everyday existence and was therefore able to offer hope. Like many from his background, Michael Meenan had grown up with no understanding of his homosexuality or any conception that God could possibly cherish him for it. "We either accepted ourselves fully or died. Mychal's example will inspire me for the rest of my life."

As a priest vowed to poverty, chastity, and obedience, Mychal Judge walked a difficult line at times. A close heterosexual friend explained that some of his woundedness was directly connected to living with the demands of a celibate and a chaste life. But at the same time he used the energy of that in loving actions for others: "I think the sexual wound, the fact of his being gay and how he should deal with it, caused him much pain. But out of his incompletion flowed a fruitful longing."

Not surprisingly, perhaps, Mychal Judge suffered bouts of depression over his sexuality, but never needed to take time off. He confided in close friends and the gay people to whom he ministered. There was at times a sense of frustration at being alone, but he did not suffer from loneliness as such. At the same time he desired greater and deeper friendships. But communal living failed to satisfy these yearnings. A religious brotherhood could be a wonderful support, but it provided no guarantee of true friendship. Father Mychal had only a few real friends within the friary. However, he would not allow his transient moments of anxiety to interfere with his responsibilities. Always aware that public knowledge of his sexual identity could undermine his work, he invariably kept quiet because he did not want homophobia to compromise his ministry. Neither did he wish to alienate people or challenge their prejudices too directly. His style was to try gently to encourage them to accept difference in whatever shape they encountered it. Many firefighters tacitly understood he was gay and respected his privacy.

There were friends away from West Thirty-first Street with whom he could share his story. Father Brendan O'Rourke, rector of Clonard Monastery in Belfast, Northern Ireland, trained and worked as a pastoral psychotherapist in New York for ten years. He said that Mychal Judge did not need to hide any part of himself once he was in company he could trust. What struck him about Mychal was how he managed to balance a lot of opposing forces within him and yet remain free. He had come to terms with being gay and disagreed with official church teaching about gay orientation and gay relationships.

Having grown up in a repressive seminary world at a time when homosexuality was a criminal offense, Mychal Judge lived through times of extraordinary transformation both in society and within himself. But he carried the scars and bore the tensions of someone at the crossroads of sexuality and spirituality: of being gay, a priest, and a Franciscan; of being Catholic, gay, and Irish. He was a compendium of identities. Many in his situation might have walked away from the church and become spiritually disillusioned or psychologically unstable.

Mychal Judge stayed and took risks. When Brendan Fay organized the city's first inclusive St. Patrick's parade in Queens in March 2000, Mychal Judge marched in it, as did Hillary Clinton. The theme was "Cherishing All the Children of the Nation Equally." He was hesitant initially, Fay admitted:

> Mychal and I would be speaking twice a week and he'd be asking: "How's the parade going? How are the plans going? Great! Great!" He supported it financially. As the day approached, there was an understanding between us that he might not be able to come.
>
> But then I saw him turn up in his habit and sandals — and he joined in. He walked along the route as a group of angry protesters, holding up rosary beads and crucifixes, screamed from the sidelines. Mychal just looked at them, smiled, gave them a blessing or waved. He would always say, "Resentments will do us in." He lived by that and people saw that. He wasn't angry or resentful in return. He looked on these people more with pity and compassion. He affirmed people along the way. He spent time with children.
>
> I was rushing around, and he came and looked for me, put his hand on my shoulder, and prayed. That was Mychal Judge — bringing a prayerful presence to this historic moment.

One observer remembered Father Mychal "speaking softly" with a man and woman who had remonstrated with him for marching. A heterosexual friend told me that Father Mychal's participation that day had been another example of the priest's heroism, an act of solidarity that had resulted in "an appreciation almost beyond description." The gay community felt so marginalized and rejected by the church that to have Mychal Judge there, as its visible and unequivocal presence, spoke of the man's nobility: "To celebrate their Irishness and their gayness in such a public manner took a lot of guts, as it did to go to the World Trade Center on September 11 and stay there. It took guts for him to go to the special interest groups within A.A., where he was able to meet other gay men in recovery. There he felt comfortable with himself. He was in touch with his feelings. His courage was a spiritual courage."

Brendan Fay suggested chastity had been as much a struggle for Mychal Judge as it had been for many of his Franciscan brothers. He had joined the community at a time when homosexuality was taboo. There were moments in his life when he needed to explore, to think, and to find himself. Within his own A.A. community, Mychal Judge had begun a journey from despair to hope, from self-rejection to self-acceptance. Gradually he had moved to a place of recognizing that being gay was a gift as opposed to a burden, wound, or handicap — a gift of God and a gift of himself.

"Many never make it that far," Fay said:

> Other priests deal with it in different ways. Mychal would speak about acceptance and gift. Never did I hear him speak about being gay as being a burden or a cross. He would say, "It's wonderful, wonderful, wonderful. Look at who we are as gay people at this moment in history, as being a gift for the church, to witness change and be agents for change both in church and society."

But there were also times when he was less exuberant about his sexuality. He knew that he hadn't managed to integrate it completely. Nonetheless, he always found ways through the darkness and was the first to look down at his own feet of clay.

Brother Thomas, of the Society of St. Francis, recalled Judge voicing frustration about the church's prejudice against gay people. He made it clear to Brother Thomas that he was "deeply pained" by the roadblocks. He never knew him to hide his homosexuality, especially when ministering to people with HIV or AIDS. They were the beloved children of God. They had no reason to believe their orientation made them sinners. "I always thought he was a man of courage," said Brother Thomas. "I thought he was a man of tremendous integrity, particularly in the way he handled his sexuality and his genuine manner with other people. But he told me he had gone through periods of depression in his recovery as an alcoholic and had had rough times."

The private journals of Mychal Judge reveal that the Franciscan longed to be more open with certain friends but had intuited from his conversations with them that they might not be comfortable with this truth. For Father Mychal, it was *their* feelings — not his — that mattered most. Like many gay people, he could be honest about every other aspect of his life but feared causing offense or risking rejection. He knew how the gay issue could divide families and communities in unpredictable ways. There was a certain ambiguity about Father Mychal's own position as an openly gay Franciscan. He was always worried he might be asked to relinquish his priesthood. He talked at times about becoming "a gay man in retirement." His journey toward full authenticity was complicated but he was always honestly seeking the courage to be himself, an understated form of heroism that strengthened him for the trials ahead.

19

LOVESCAPE CRUCIFIED

———⊶⊷———

Joy fall to thee, father Francis,
Drawn to the Life that died;
With the gnarls of the nails in thee, niche of the lance, his
Lovescape crucified
And seal of his seraph-arrival! and these thy daughters
And five-livèd and leavèd favour and pride,
Are sisterly sealed in wild waters,
To bathe in his fall-gold mercies, to breathe in his all-fire glances

—Gerard Manley Hopkins,
from *The Wreck of the Deutschland*

F RANCIS'S LOVE FOR PEOPLE grew as he spent more and more
time praying. Sometimes his joy in remembering Jesus Christ
kept him awake at nights. One September day, on the eve of the
feast of the Cross, the saint was praying secretly in his cell when,
according to *The Little Flowers*, an angel appeared to him and said
on God's behalf: "I encourage you and urge you to prepare and
dispose yourself humbly to receive with all patience what God
wills to do in you."

Francis answered: "I am prepared to endure patiently whatever
my Lord wants to do to me." The angel departed. The following
day, Francis arose before dawn and began to pray outside the
entrance of his cell, turning his face toward the east:

My Lord Jesus Christ, I pray You to grant me two graces
before I die: the first is that during my life I may feel in my
soul and in my body, as much as possible, that pain which
You, dear Jesus, sustained in the hour of Your most bitter

Passion. The second is that I may feel in my heart, as much as possible, that excessive love with which You, O Son of God, were inflamed in willingly enduring such suffering for us sinners.

Remaining in prayer for a long period, he understood that God would grant his requests "and that it should be soon conceded to him to feel those things as much as it is possible." Having received the promise, St. Francis began to contemplate "with intense devotion the Passion of Christ and his infinite charity." The fervor of his devotion increased so much within him that he "utterly transformed himself into Jesus through love and compassion."

And while he was "thus inflaming himself in this contemplation," on that same morning he saw coming down from heaven a Seraph with six resplendent and flaming wings. As the Seraph, flying swiftly, came closer to St. Francis, he noticed he had the likeness of a Crucified Man, and his wings were so disposed that two extended above his head, two were spread out to fly, and the other two covered his entire body. St. Francis was afraid but also filled with joy, grief, and amazement. He was reported to have felt intense joy from the kindly gaze of Christ. But seeing the figure nailed to the cross, he felt "boundless grief and compassion." He was astounded at such an extraordinary vision for he knew well that the affliction of suffering was not in accord with the immortality of the angelic Seraph. "And while he was marveling thus, he who was appearing to him revealed to him that this vision was shown to him by Divine Providence in this particular form in order that he should understand that he was to be utterly transformed into the direct likeness of Christ Crucified not by physical martyrdom, but by enkindling of the mind."

According to early sources, Francis himself bore in his body five wounds, the stigmata of Christ. His hands and feet were punctured right through as if by nails and still bore their black scars. His side looked as if it had been pierced by a lance and often shed blood. Francis took care to ensure that the marks, which never fully healed over the course of two years, should be kept secret except to the very few who cared for him. He asked God for the same pain that Christ had experienced on the cross so that he could better understand and feel the same love Christ felt for humankind. It is the first recorded instance of such stigmata. Three hundred cases have since been reported, including that of the Franciscan friar Padre Pio, who died in 1968 and was canonized in June 2002.

THERE WERE NO SUCH MARKS on the body of Mychal Judge. However, in the light of his death — itself a modern "Lovescape Crucified" — William Hart McNichols told me how he believed the wounds of Father Mychal's life had brought a seraphic love to others. Father McNichols, an iconographer in New Mexico, has made a careful study of St. Francis and the stigmata and produced an icon of the seraphic encounter for the Church of San Francisco de Asís in Ranchos de Taos. The Byzantine-style image reveals St. Francis illuminated by moonlight from a Taos mountain, Pueblo Peak. Mychal Judge, whom he first encountered at a Mass for healing, is to be one of his future subjects.

Because St. Francis had never wounded people, he had received the stigmata, said Father McNichols. St. Francis was described as an *alter Christus*, another Christ. He wanted to experience the pain that Jesus had experienced on the cross. He had been rejected by the church he had been sent to reform and ostracized from the world he had come to evangelize. St. Francis wanted to know how Christ could love people so much after what they had done to him. St. Francis received both the wounds and the seraphic love in which no one had been bathed before.

Mychal Judge lived out of this vision. He was wounded with the wounds that the world had given him. Father McNichols commented: "When wounds are accepted or even healed, they become sources of healing for others. Seraphic love is the joy of being healed in motion. It is a sign of resurrection after crucifixion. You are finally free, free to love completely without any fear

and to care for other people. Like St. Francis, you move around
with your wounds and this was what Mychal Judge did."

In his later years Mychal Judge faced his own physical wounds.
His health began to deteriorate and, while he never lost his good
looks, he aged noticeably. He suffered several serious illnesses and
underwent surgery. He was surprised that he pulled through. At
one stage he was given the wrong medication and complications
set in. He said he was prepared for a sudden and happy death.
He joked that he did not want to end his days in a nursing home
for incontinent friars. A friend remembered visiting him when he
was forced to sacrifice his role as grand marshal in the St. Patrick's
Day Parade for a hospital bed. There was a lot of anxiety that he
might not have made a good recovery.

When I arrived in the hospital room his hands were joined.
I was slightly alarmed because it looked as if he had been
laid out. He was lying with his mouth slightly open but his
hands joined in front of him. When I introduced myself and
we started chatting, he said, "Oh, I have just been away
with the Lord." The Lord was able perhaps to speak to him
in his heart. I'm not sure how comfortable he was with that
because he always liked to have the last word!

The year before he died, he remarked that making decisions at
sixty-seven was not the same as thinking about them at thirty-
seven. He said he prayed all the time for guidance on how to
make decisions.

I don't know what's next for me. I've had the best life of any
friar in this house or of any priest I know. It's great to be a
Franciscan. I take the ups and downs, the joys and sorrows,
but that's life and I try to keep them balanced. I get down
on my knees and pray, "Lord, help me." I have to get God
in there because it's his world and he loves us and wants to
hear from us. There are so many great things in my life. I
have a wonderful, wonderful, wonderful, fruitful life — but

I work at it and I pray continuously. I have to work at it because life is a mystery. I pray, "Lord, show me, take me, mold me, fashion me, show me what you want. I watch and listen, and it will come."

Like other Franciscans, he had been given a sheet of paper entitled "On the Occasion of Your Death" on which he had been asked to give details of the readings and music he would like at his funeral, as well as names of people to take part. Mychal Judge had approached a number of priest friends and asked if they would be prepared to speak at his own Requiem Mass, occupying a role he himself had played at many funerals and one he would have even liked to assume at his own. There was always the frustration that he wouldn't be able to preach and reminisce at his own farewell. He asked Stephen Weaver if he would be prepared to speak specifically about the European dimension of his life, partly, Weaver suspects, to show that the boy from Brooklyn did have a capacity for an appreciation of beauty, art, and civilization. He was keen for people to know that he had explored within European culture the wonder of creation and human ingenuity inspired by God and he wanted such a consideration brought to bear in that moment of remembrance of him.

On the fortieth anniversary of his ordination to the priesthood, February 25, 2001, he wrote a letter of gratitude to his family and friends.

It is almost midnight and the day is done. Today was the 40th anniversary of my priesthood — 1961 — and the cold rainy day was an exact replica of the day in Washington when Archbishop Vagnozzi, the Apostolic Delegate, laid his hands firmly on my head and gifted me with priesthood. Glorious!

Someone asked me today if I had any idea, at all, what lay ahead of me on that day. I knew I would say Mass and preach, that I would baptize, bury the dead, and perform weddings. The rest was all in the hands of God. I could never have dreamt of all the parish years I would enjoy;

the lively days in the dorm at Siena College; the extraordinary challenging year at Canterbury, England; the filling and
emptying of the clothes closet for the homeless; the blessed
ministry to the sick and dying with the AIDS virus; and now
the joyful challenge as Chaplain of the New York City Fire
Department. What a grace-filled Franciscan priesthood.

And today, over and over again, here at St. Francis, at
the two Masses I said at St. Michael's on Fourth Avenue
in Brooklyn, and during the visit I made along the way to
St. Anselm's Church in Bay Ridge, where my parents were
married, I said, "Thank You, Lord!" Through these past forty
years, you were with me along the way with your prayers,
your needs, your cards, your gifts.

And the future? As on ordination day, only God knows,
and he will reveal only what I need to know and to do each
day. It will be wonderful — that's the way God is.

I love you, bless you, and thank you.

Toward the end, Judge felt he had reached a certain conscious-
ness through the serious confrontations he had made with his
"shadow self." Many of his strengths were located within the very
weaknesses he had learned to face. His gifts were all the more
precious to people because of their wounded source. "That would
tell me there was an integration between his inner and his outer
life," said Richard Rohr. He was doing good work and he knew
he was doing it for personal reasons too, yet did not doubt this
was the way he was going to help people. Rohr did not observe
him to be frenetic but explained that overachievement could be
an indication of a certain sense of unworthiness and inability.
Overcompensation often hinted at a lack of self-esteem. Rohr
continued:

I felt I was with a calm, happy man who was doing a lot.
He suffered from issues of self-doubt throughout his life, but
I did not notice that drivenness that I often see in some
overcompensators and sometimes see in myself. I think he

would not have assumed he was an instrument of God to any great degree. I think he had a genuine relationship with God because he talked about God easily. It wasn't artificial or trumped up, and you did not have to pull it out of him. It was natural and dialogical. Although he ended up being a father figure, I think he was a happy son of God.

Through his channels of energy, many people felt the touch of God's love. Broken humanity, ever alive, was the conduit through which God was able to use him as an instrument of his peace. His heroism grew out of his vocation as a wounded healer. The love of God was not impeded in this person who was willing to give himself as he really was: a broken, incomplete man searching for total integration in the service of God's kingdom and through his love of others. Father Patrick Fitzgerald explained: "God's love did not pass through Mychal Judge in a passive way like water through a straw, but God's love took on the character of Mychal Judge. That personality wasn't perfect but it was a perfect instrument for God."

In June 2001, more than two hundred Franciscans gathered 140 miles north of New York City to celebrate the hundredth anniversary of Holy Name Province at Friar Tuck Inn in the Catskill Mountains. It was the occasion of the "Chapter of Mats" that originated at one of first meetings around 1220 when all the world's friars assembled at Assisi and brought their mats with them. At the Holy Name celebration one of the friars was seriously ill with cancer and knew time was short. Doctors had told him there was nothing more they could do. Mychal Judge had talked privately about the friar's courage and his imminent passing from this world. Turning to two of his brothers, Mychal commented that you have to go the way God wants you to go but that he certainly hoped he would not die of a lingering illness. His hope was that when his time came, he would depart this life quickly.

The day before his death, Father Mychal traveled to a firehouse in the Bronx to rededicate the house after major renovation and say Mass. Those who were present felt, in retrospect, that his words were valedictory:

> We come to this house this morning to celebrate renewal, rejuvenation, new life. We come to thank God for the blessings of all the years that the good work has been done here and especially the last few days. We can never thank God enough for the reality of the lives we have. So standing in his presence this morning — and truly this is a chapel — let us pause for a moment, perhaps close our eyes and thank God for some special blessing in our individual lives. You do what God has called you to do...you go out to do the job which is a mystery and a surprise.... No matter how big the call, no matter how small, you have no idea what God's calling you to but he needs you. He needs me. He needs all of us. He needs your prayers.... Those of you who are working now, keep going. Keep supporting each other. Be kind to each other. Love each other. Work together...and from this house, God's blessings go forth to this community. It's fantastic but very painful. We love the job. We all do. What a blessing that is — a difficult, difficult job, and God calls you to it and indeed he gives you a love for it so that a difficult job will be well done. Isn't he a wonderful guy? Isn't he good to you, to each one of you, and to me? Turn to him each day, put your faith and your trust and your hope and your life in his hands. And he'll take care of you. And you'll have a good life. And this house will be a great, great blessing to this neighborhood and to this city. Amen.

Friends agreed he would have viewed with irony his death less than twenty-four hours later. "For him to die that way — that was typical Mike Judge," said Malachy McCourt.

> The design of it! He just wanted to go like that — a hero — but he didn't want to be a saint. It was too much of a burden. He was a hero in life in the sense that he looked after people.

He flew around the city with those robes flying in all kinds of weather, without socks. The man had some kind of power to be in two or three places at once. He was the omnipresent spiritual New Yorker, the best of this city. But I think he would have been vastly uncomfortable with the international publicity surrounding his death. He would never think of himself as anything but a humble friar. He was the ultimate servant of God and of people.

Frank Murphy believed the importance of his death lay in the fact that he was doing exactly what he thought he was there for — attending to the spiritual and moral needs of New Yorkers. After the planes crashed into the World Trade Center, he showed no hesitancy in being present: "I am sure he realized that he was in danger of losing his life — that was what Mychal Judge did."

Mychal McNicholas sensed he would have forgiven the terrorists who attacked on September 11:

And he would have been uneasy about the war rhetoric that followed. He would say the attackers had done a terrible thing and should be brought to justice, but he would still have asked God to forgive them. He lived his life based on the gospel text: "Love one another as I have loved you." That was his beauty.

September 11, 2001, was the apogee of Father Mychal Judge's remarkable ministry. For him the cross represented the place of God's most intimate engagement with the world. What else would he have done but anoint a man and lay himself open to death? The parallels drawn that day between Mychal Judge and the figure of Christ were not romantic metaphors. He was indeed the victim who saved. In that sense he could be rightly claimed as a hero. In any event, the notion of heavenly life or the beatific vision had always informed his perspective of everyday life in New York. Stephen Weaver told me:

His passage from the apocalyptic moments at the base of the twin towers to his sharing the presence of God with the angels and saints was so swift that it strikes me as being typically Mychal. I entertain the fantasy that if he did take off his helmet to anoint the fireman, it was with a nod toward Francis and all the other saintly figures. I sensed this was an action that nudged him over that threshold. There would have been very little resistance to his letting go of his earthly ministry and embracing the company of the saints.

Stephen Weaver felt Mychal Judge would have needed to take off the helmet. It was "a wonderfully Christlike image" in the manner of Jesus allowing himself to be fully present to his own tormentors and the destructive forces that surrounded him at the end of his earthly ministry. "Mychal entered into that moment bareheaded with only his faith as a thin membrane separating him from Sister Death."

WHEN IT CAME, the funeral of Father Mychal Judge was a much more spectacular event than he could have imagined. A two-day viewing of the body in St. Francis's lower church culminated in a wake service led by the pastor, Father Peter Brophy. Among those attending were Mayor Rudolph Giuliani, Fire Commissioner Thomas Von Essen, and New York Governor George Pataki. Giuliani commented: "Father Mychal is now up in heaven with Cardinal O'Connor, and O'Connor is letting him say Mass."

The following morning, Saturday, September 15 — what would have been the twenty-third anniversary of Mychal Judge's sobriety — nearly three thousand people packed the main church and overflowed into the lower church. Outside a crowd on Thirty-first Street followed the Mass on television screens. There were firefighters in smart uniforms and others caked in grime who had come straight from rescue work at Ground Zero. One remarked: "I just think God wanted somebody to lead the guys to heaven."

The archbishop of New York, Cardinal Edward Egan, was the principal celebrant of the Mass of Christian Burial. In the congregation were former President Bill Clinton, his wife, U.S. Senator Hillary Rodham Clinton, and their daughter, Chelsea. Speaking at the Mass, Senator Clinton recalled Mychal Judge's presence sitting next to her at a presidential prayer breakfast: "He lit up the White House," she said. Father Judge's chosen homilist was Father Michael Duffy, director of St. Francis Inn, Philadelphia. He commented that, after the international tributes that had been paid to Mychal Judge in the days after September 11, the preacher at Mother Teresa's funeral must have had an easier task. The Good Shepherd had laid down his life for the sheep. Greater love than this no man had than to lay down his life for his friends. Father Duffy continued:

> Mychal Judge has always been my friend. And now he is my hero. Mychal Judge's body was the first one released from Ground Zero. His death certificate has the number one on the top. . . . Why was Mychal Judge number one? . . . Mychal's goal and purpose in life at that time was to bring the firemen to the point of death so they would be ready to meet their maker. There are between two and three hundred firemen buried there, the commissioner told us last night. Mychal Judge could not have ministered to them all. It was physically impossible in this life but not in the next. And I think that, if he were given his choice, he would prefer to have happened what actually happened. He passed through the other side of life, and now he can continue doing what he wanted to do with all his heart. And the next few weeks, we're going to have names added, name after name of people who are being brought out of that rubble. And Mychal Judge is going to be on the other side of death . . . to greet them instead of sending them there. And he's going to greet them with that big Irish smile. . . . He's going to take them by the arm and say, "Welcome. I want to take you to my father. . . ."

We come to bury Mike Judge's body but not his spirit. We come to bury his mind but not his dreams. We come to bury his voice but not his message. We come to bury his hands but not his good works. We come to bury his heart but not his love. Never his love.

Father Duffy told the congregation that, as they had all felt Mychal Judge's big hands through a blessing, they should give him a blessing as he returned to God. He asked the mourners to stand, raise their right hands, and extend them toward the coffin:

Father Duffy: Mychal, may the Lord bless you.

Congregation: Mychal, may the Lord bless you.

Father Duffy: May the angels lead you to your Savior.

Congregation: May the angels lead you to your Savior.

Father Duffy: You are a sign of his presence to us.

Congregation: You are a sign of his presence to us.

Father Duffy: May the Lord now embrace you.

Congregation: May the Lord now embrace you.

Father Duffy: And hold you in his love forever.

Congregation: And hold you in his love forever.

Father Duffy: Rest in Peace, Amen.

Congregation: Rest in Peace, Amen.

The casket was carried out of the church by firefighters. Interment was in the friars' plot at Holy Sepulchre Cemetery, Totowa, New Jersey.

COMMUNITIES AROUND THE WORLD honored those who had died. At the Lyceum Theater in London's West End, where Roger Wright was starring as Simba in *The Lion King,* a minute's silence was observed for those who lost their lives. During the week the cast and backstage crew raised money for the American Red Cross, spearheaded each night by a speech from one of the principal

actors. Later that week, after the final curtain, Roger walked to
the front and spoke about his friendship with Mychal Judge, the
man who had made him welcome when he was a stranger in New
York. "It was quite emotional, but I got through it. Mychal had in
fact been to the show earlier that year."

Father Anthony McNeill, meanwhile, was only just recovering
from his own brush with death. Three days before September 11
he had been flying in a small Cessna, which crashed into mountains in Italy. That evening he had instinctively thought of Mychal
Judge. He even considered phoning him to tell him that he had
felt that God had blessed him that day. "I wanted to share that
spiritual experience because, in times of crisis, Mychal was the
person I phoned to get a second opinion on what was happening," he said. "But it wasn't easy to call him from Italy. After the
towers went down, I had a dual sense of guilt: the guilt I hadn't
called him and the guilt that I had survived but Mychal had died
three days later. I was given my life back and his was taken."

A world of friendships was in mourning, some of them less
publicly expressed. But for the community on West Thirty-first
Street, one of their beloved friars had gone. Father Brian Jordan, director of the Immigration Center at St. Francis of Assisi
Church, reflected on his first meeting with Mychal Judge a quarter of a century earlier on the campus of Siena College when he
had been challenged by Father Mychal about his vocation. "Forget
about becoming an unhappy lawyer," he had told him. "Become
a happy priest." Brian Jordan had never forgotten those words.
Father Mychal had constantly encouraged young men to consider
a vocation to the religious life and the priesthood. He had been
a great role model in the spirit of St. Francis. He had diagnosed
people's pain and guided them to inner strength through Franciscan prayer. He had been their anchor. He had trusted in the
goodwill of people but, most of all, had given and received love.
The proof had been his funeral.

20

AUTHENTIC AMERICAN HERO

⚬⚬⚬

S INCE HIS DEATH, Father Mychal Judge, O.F.M., has received
a succession of posthumous honors. While the pope blessed
his white chaplain's helmet in Rome, Father Mike was among
three "knights of the New York Fire Department" to be awarded
the Legion of Honor by the French president Jacques Chirac.
Presented to Father Mychal's sister, Dympna, it is France's high-
est national order. Its few American recipients include Dwight
Eisenhower and Neil Armstrong. There have been religious prizes
from colleges and universities and an international award from
the Foundation for Moral Courage. He was named Grand Marshal of the St. Patrick's Parade in Chicago as well as Irish Man
of the Year. A New York Waterway ferry was christened *Father
Mychal Judge*. The street outside the friary and firehouse has been
renamed "Father Mychal F. Judge Street."

The friar has also been awarded a number of doctorates, a gesture that would have both honored and amused a person who
yearned to be more academic. Siena College, where he once
worked, announced a Mychal Judge Scholarship for sons and
daughters of firefighters killed in the tragedy, while the Mychal
Judge Fund, administered by the Franciscans, provided emergency
short-term financial assistance to those suffering loss or injury as
a result of September 11. It had a particular and appropriate focus
on those "not included in established categories — those who had
fallen through the cracks" but whose needs were no less real.

Thomas Sciacca, a freelance illustrator in Kansas City, Mis-
souri, was "moved beyond all words" when he learned the priest
had died. Before he had even grasped his name or read about his

ministry, he instinctively knew he had to honor him. So he painted a portrait of Father Mychal and presented it to the firehouse. It is dedicated also to fallen firefighters Daniel Brethel, Andrew Desperito, Michael Weinburg, Stephen Belson, and the brothers and families of Engine 1/Ladder 24. "It is equally dedicated to all of those who live by the code of agape," he told me.

Back in County Leitrim, John Keaney started planning a memorial using a large pebble from the original Judge farmhouse. Meanwhile, a U.S. company that began manufacturing charity wristbands engraved with the name of World Trade Center heroes found itself inundated with requests for copies in memory of Mychal Judge.

DICTIONARIES DESCRIBE A HERO as someone distinguished by exceptional nobility and fortitude, a being of extraordinary strength and courage. Mychal Judge was undoubtedly that. But he was also a hero in a less dramatic sense. Environmentalist Peter Garrett, deemed a hero for his work in promoting land rights in Australia, once defined heroism as "a core set of values, which include thinking about and doing things for others, self-belief without boasting, the capacity to accept setbacks without giving in, and a sense of humility." These words certainly apply to Mychal Judge.

Some activists were quick to label Mychal Judge a "gay hero" in the days after the tragedy. But as the writer Andrew Sullivan was equally swift to recognize, he had died doing what he had always done — tending to his flock. Sullivan insisted: "He is not a gay hero. He is an American hero who was also gay."

Many people, gay and straight alike, pointed out that Mychal Judge's sexuality was subordinate to his unique witness as a priest and a Franciscan. He ministered across the spectrum of city life and was nonexclusive in his care. What marked out his holiness was precisely his refusal to inhabit any niche of conventional sanctity. Just as Francis had challenged the church of his day and become a saint, so Mychal Judge is emerging as a hero of the post-Christian era. For here was a friar who dared to be himself. He found the moral courage to own his unique identity in a church that preferred more traditional affiliation — and in a society at times grown cynical about the exercise of priestly ministry.

It was undoubtedly a more dangerous path and, time and again, it led him into the eye of the storm, right up to the morning of September 11, when his courage received its ultimate test. In the company of "New York's bravest," Father Mychal Judge died as he had lived: an authentic American hero.

BLESSING

―∞―

Mychal's Prayer

Lord, take me where you want me to go;
Let me meet who you want me to meet;
Tell me what you want me to say,
and
Keep me out of Your way.

—Father Mychal Judge, O.F.M.
(1933–2001)

BIBLIOGRAPHY

Books

Adam, David. *The Edge of Glory: Prayers in the Celtic Tradition.* Wilton, Conn.: Morehouse-Barlow, 1988; London: Triangle/SPCK, 1989.

Arnold, Johann Christoph. *Be Not Afraid: Overcoming the Fear of Death.* Farmington, Pa.: Plough Publishing House, 2002.

Beattie, Melody. *The Language of Letting Go: Daily Meditations for Codependents.* Center City, Minn.: Hazelden Foundation, 1990.

Cousins, E., trans. *Bonaventure.* Classics of Western Spirituality. New York and Mahwah, N.J.: Paulist Press, 1978.

De Mello, Anthony. *The Way to Love: The Last Meditations of Anthony de Mello.* New York: Doubleday Image, 1995.

Downey, Michael, ed. *The New Dictionary of Catholic Spirituality.* Collegeville, Minn.: Liturgical Press, 1993.

Ellis, Edward Robb. *The Epic of New York City.* New York: Kodansha International, 1997.

Farina, John, ed. *Beauty for Ashes: Spiritual Reflections on the Attack on America.* New York: Crossroad, 2001.

Ford, Michael. *Wounded Prophet: A Portrait of Henri J. M. Nouwen.* New York: Doubleday Image, 2002.

French, R. M., trans. *The Way of a Pilgrim.* London: Triangle/SPCK, 1995.

Gallagher, Jim. *Padre Pio: The Pierced Priest.* London: Fount, 1995.

Habig, Marion A., ed. *St. Francis of Assisi: Writings and Early Biographies, English Omnibus of the Sources for the Life of St. Francis.* Chicago: Franciscan Herald Press, 1972.

Hazelden Foundation. *The Twelve Steps of Alcoholics Anonymous.* Center City, Minn.: Hazelden Foundation, 1993.

Heywood, W., ed. *The Little Flowers of St. Francis of Assisi.* New York: Random House, 1998.

House, Adrian. *Francis of Assisi.* New York and Mahwah, N.J.: Paulist Press, 2002.

Keenan, James F., S.J., ed., with Jon D. Fuller, S.J., Lisa Sowle Cahill, and Kevin Kelly. *Catholic Ethicists on HIV/AIDS Prevention.* New York: Continuum International, 2000.

Knox, Ronald, trans. *Autobiography of a Saint, Therese of Lisieux.* London: Fount Paperbacks, 1979.

Lynch, Father Bernard. *A Priest on Trial.* London: Bloomsbury, 1993.

May, Gerald G., *Addiction and Grace.* San Francisco: HarperSan-Francisco, 1991.

McCourt, Malachy. *Danny Boy: The Beloved Irish Ballad.* Philadelphia: Running Press, 2002.

McDonald, Steven, and Patti Ann McDonald, with E. J. Kahn III. *The Steven McDonald Story.* New York: Donald I. Fine, 1989.

McNeill, John J. *The Church and the Homosexual.* Boston: Beacon Press, 1993.

Monahan, Sister Molly. *Seeds of Grace: A Nun's Reflections on the Spirituality of Alcoholics Anonymous.* New York: Riverhead Books, 2001.

Mushabac, Jane, and Angela Wigan. *A Short and Remarkable History of New York City.* New York: Fordham University Press, 1999.

Nouwen, Henri J. M. *The Wounded Healer.* New York: Image Books, 1990; London: Darton, Longman and Todd, 1994.

O'Donohue, John. *Anam Cara.* New York: Bantam Press, 1998.

Sister Nan, C.S.F., ed. *The Message of St. Francis.* New York: Penguin Studio, 1999.

Smith, Dennis. *Report from Ground Zero: The Story of the Rescue Efforts at the World Trade Center.* New York: Viking Penguin, 2002.

Articles

Ballner, Patricia. "Dialogue with a Friar." *The Agony and the Ecstasy* 1, no. 5 (October 4, 2000).

Carven, Frank. "Father Mychal Judge, O.F.M." *Harford County Attorney's Legal Newsletter,* November 2001.

Duffy, Father Michael. "Funeral Homily for Father Mychal Judge," September 15, 2001. Available at the Franciscan Holy Name Province website, *www.hnp.org.*

Feister, John Bookser, and John Zawadzinski. "No Greater Love." *St. Anthony Messenger,* December 2001.

Gianopoulos, Janet. "Fire in the Sky, Fallout on Earth." Holy Name Province Special Report, July 22, 1996.

Luhrs, Claire. "A Flock of Franciscans." *West Milford Argus,* November 18, 1984.

McGoldrick, Debbie. "The Fr. Judge I Knew and Loved." *Irish Voice,* March 13, 2002.

Senior, Jennifer. "The Firemen's Friar." *New York Metro – New York Magazine,* November 12, 2001.

Supik, Wilma. "The Listening Priest." *Bergen Sunday Record,* September 8, 1974.

Videos

The Church of St. Francis of Assisi — The Heart of New York. Globe Video Services, Inc., 2001.

"Fr. Mychal Judge in Northern Ireland." Unpublished video footage. Bruderhof Video Productions, Ulster Park, N.Y.

9.11. CBS. March 2002.

Songs of Praise — from New York, BBC1, December 16, 2001.